Christina Stead's The Man Who Loved Children:
Bookmarked

Christina Stead's
The Man Who Loved Children

BOOKMARKED

LUCY FERRISS

New York, NY

Ig Publishing
Box 2547
New York, NY 10163
www.igpub.com

ISBN: 978-1-63246-154-4

PRINTED IN THE UNITED STATES OF AMERICA

FIRST EDITION | FIRST PRINTING

For Don, who knows how to love

When I was thirteen, I was tall for my age but young for my class in school. I had skipped fifth grade. My youth and my school success were a pair of deep embarrassments for me, and while my home life was far from calm, I had enjoyed for a while the illusion that there, at least, I could wear my ambitions on my sleeve; I could set aside my pimply face, my overlarge nose, my general ugliness; I could open the invisible door of my cage. Then, one day, I was preparing to go to some sort of party, or maybe to one of the excruciating ballroom dance classes my brother and I attended to prepare ourselves for lives teetering on America's upper crust. I had curled the ends of my hair, and my mother had allowed me a swipe of her mascara. After examining my face in the hallway mirror, I trotted into the kitchen to announce that I thought I had discovered in my reflection some resemblance to a

TV character, maybe Marlo Thomas. My father laughed. Would you believe, he asked my mother, who was washing the dishes, that this girl thinks she's a movie star? I burst into tears, a bad habit I couldn't seem to break, and fled the room as my mother interrupted my father's chuckles with sharp words. He was teasing, my father kept saying. Couldn't the girl take a little joke?

I don't remember when I first encountered Christina Stead's masterpiece, *The Man Who Loved Children*. My much-annotated edition dates from 1980, fifteen years after the critic Randall Jarrell's endorsement returned the book to print following its mediocre initial rollout in 1940. During most of my teaching career, whenever the design of a college course lent itself to including the novel on the syllabus, I fit it in. The students found its villain, Sam Pollit, charming at first and loathsome as they read on. It was the one book that prompted both male and female students to ask for a conference, shut the door to my office, and pour out their grief over their family. At one point, when the book was (again) out of stock, I managed to reach its current editor, who told me that only the writer Robb Forman Dew and I were keeping the title in print by teaching it. More recently, Jonathan Franzen's rousing *New York Times* endorsement of the book returned it once more to readers. In 2010 it was listed as one of *Times's* "All-Time 100 Novels." Still, it's fair to say that among serious readers for whom names like Djuna Barnes, Carson McCullers, Richard Yates, and Dawn Powell all ring a bell, the name Christina Stead means nothing.

I'm certain that the novel looms large for me because I am both a daughter and a writer. Very few *Künstlerromanen*, books narrating the maturation of an artist, exist for women. The ones that do, like Alcott's *Little Women*, focus at least as much on the marriage plot as on the development of the artist. Perhaps even more salient, I know something of what it's like to grow up with a father twisted by what I can only call the toxic masculinity of the 1930s, which differs in some ways but not entirely from a self-regarding masculinity that has tormented daughters, wives, and men themselves for centuries and has nowhere been described so honestly or in full as in *The Man Who Loved Children*.

The two best-known fans of the book are both male writers. I find their descriptions of what Stead accomplishes remarkably different from what female critics have had to say about the book. I'm going to begin by taking a hard look at those differences before

I dig further into how the book itself has found echoes in my life and the way I think about my work. Stead's subject matters, and her character-building leaves me in awe, but she also offers writers like me a challenging road map in terms of style in its largest sense—that is, as a way of conceiving what a novel should be; what a novel can do; and what we're up against, both in our writing process and in our careers, if we try to do the form justice.

Christina Stead was born in 1902 in Australia, which she left in 1928 for Europe and then America. Always sensitive about her looks and her attractiveness to men, she lived with and eventually married a gregarious, cosmopolitan, Marxist financier whose fortunes rose and fell through the Depression. Her early books—*Seven Poor Men of Sydney* (1934), *The Beauties and Furies* (1936), and *House of All Nations* (1938)—concerned relationships among and between adult men and women, with the same rich, strange gift for characterization as in *The Man Who Loved Children*, but without obvious autobiography or any focus on coming of age. Her overall viewpoint was socialist, with a keen awareness of how class, capitalism, politics and money affect our deepest desires and relationships. When she finally dug into her own past to write *The Man*

Who Loved Children, the eighteen months of composition were confirmation of Red Smith's purported maxim, "There's nothing to writing. You just sit at a typewriter and open a vein." According to Stead's biographer, Hazel Rowley, "The memories came flooding back. She slept badly. She raged. She wept."[1]

The plot of the book, relocated at Simon & Schuster's request from Sydney, Australia, to Washington, D.C., and from the early twentieth century to the late 1930s, centers on Stead's alter ego, Louisa Pollit, known as Louie, eleven years old at the start of the novel and fourteen when she escapes home at its end. Following the death of Rachel, Louie's sweet, religious mother, her father, Samuel Pollit, married Henrietta "Henny" Collyer, the youngest daughter of a prominent Washington insider. Louie has no full siblings, but at the novel's opening, Sam and Henrietta have brought five offspring into the household—Ernie, whose anxieties express themselves through earning and hoarding money; the twins, Saul and Sam Jr., whom Sam Sr. enjoys setting on each other in fistfights; the angelic Evie, the only other girl; and Tommy, Henny's "little kissing-bug." Midway through, following an act of conception that makes sense only as a strategic exchange of power, a sixth baby, Charles-Franklin, comes along, making for seven young Pollits.

These are the children Sam "loves," his love a smothering stew of baby talk; impossible family projects; and hyperbolic lectures on the perfidy of religion, the fellowship of mankind, the benefits of eugenics-inspired euthanasia, and the self-realization of boys (through violence) and girls (through marriage and motherhood). Henny despises her husband and her lot in life, and mothers her brood with a bitter, loving savagery. To Henny, Louie is initially anathema and later a fellow traveler. Louie herself, physically awkward and intellectually creative, convinced that she is a genius, alternately craves and recoils from her father's attention and his insistence that she is a carbon copy of him.

At the start of the novel, the Pollits live in a mansion allotted to them by Henny's wealthy father, David Collyer. Things begin to change when Sam, who has held his position in the government thanks to his father-in-law's reputation, embarks on a Smithsonian expedition to Malaysia. There, he manages to offend both his American superior by currying favor with the British, and his Chinese secretary (a Kuomintang agitator, as it turns out) with his cloying racism:

He walked bareheaded; he believed that his wonderful white-gold hair, rarely seen except in Friesland or Norway, protected him, that these childlike people took him for something next to a god. When Naden told him he was like a god, he saw no humor in it.

Almost immediately on Sam's return from Malaysia, two inevitabilities strike that change the course of the novel. First, Henny's father dies, leaving only "a hole in his credit" and forcing the family to quit their Georgetown mansion for Spa House, a ramshackle place on the underside of Annapolis. Second, without the protection of his father-in-law, Sam finds himself friendless in his government post and is gradually ousted from his position. As a result, "the distant and authoritarian Sam who had come home was not quite the lighthearted Sam that had gone away; he was harsher, and a European, he had the germ power in his brain." The lack of money, always an issue in the household, rises to the fore in Henny's and Sam's fights, particularly with a newborn in the squalid home.

Louie finds relief from the unending misery of her parents by writing plays, inventing languages, reading Shelley and Milton, befriending her equally brilliant and even poorer schoolmate Clare, and composing poems to Miss Aiden, the teacher on whom she has a crush. As Sam tries to instruct Louie about her sexual future, the ambivalence she's shown toward him hardens into antipathy, even hatred. The only other girl in the family, Evie (Sam's "Little Womey"), is compliant and feminine but afflicted with enormous anxiety that seems to anticipate the position she'll find herself in once Louie leaves home. Around the Pollits swirl disturbing harbingers. The childless, querulous neighbors whom Louie visits ask her to do them a "favor" by killing their cat. Elsewhere in the neighborhood, a father is arrested for raping and impregnating his eleven-year-old daughter. Miss Aiden comes to visit and finds "poverty that to her was actually incredible." In a burst of egotistical energy, Sam sets all the children to a days-long project of boiling a marlin caught by a neighbor, in hope of skimming off and selling the noxious oil.

Murder and suicide haunt the book, from Louie's willingness to euthanize the neighbors' cat to Sam's description of a utopia in which "murder of the unfit, incurable, and insane" would be "beautiful," to Henny's gossip with her mother and sister on the various means by which a woman can kill herself. After a late-night fight between the parents culminates in Sam's raping Henny, Henny quickly disintegrates. Her extramarital affair falls apart. She is so desperate for money that she raids her hoarding son Ernie's tiny stash, and Ernie in despair hangs an effigy of himself from his bedpost. Louie determines that the only solution to the family's woes is to kill both Sam and Henny. When she laces tea with cyanide, however, she panics and dumps all the poisoned tea into a single cup. Grabbing it, Henny knowingly swallows the poison and falls dead. Louie confesses to the disbelieving Sam and leaves home to seek her lonely fortune.

Though Stead had been recognized as an extraordinarily talented writer before her autobiographical novel came out, *The Man Who Loved Children* was not treated kindly by reviewers. Clifton Fadiman, who had called Stead "a simon-pure genius" in his rave review of her third novel, *The Beauties and Furies*, wrote in the *New Yorker* that *The Man Who Loved Children* "as a whole does not come off."[2] Others were less kind, calling it "blighted," "remorselessly overblown," and to Mary McCarthy, "peculiar, breathless, overwritten, incoherent . . . like an hysterical tirade."[3] As they did with F. Scott Fitzgerald's *Great Gatsby*, critics patronizingly predicted that while this book wouldn't vault

Stead into the pantheon, she might gain her place with a few more books and some honing of her prodigious talent.

Potential, I think when I read these responses. I wonder how many writers have been instructed about the potential they should—they must—fulfill, with more discipline and hard work and attention to the requirements set by the world around them. Reviews of *The Man Who Loved Children* put me in mind of my ninth grade Latin teacher, who sat me down at the end of the semester and told me that I had earned a B in her class, but, because I should have earned an A, she was awarding me a C.

One complaint of the critics reading *The Man Who Loved Children* in 1940 has floated away on the tides of time. They thought the book was neither American enough nor true to the 1930s. They pointed out various bits of slang and syntax that proved their point. These quibbles seem unimportant now. Not that we don't know the difference between America and Australia, or between 1910 and 1939—but the world of *The Man Who Loved Children* is not the world we live in, except in the ways that it is this world and always will be, so long as there are cruel fathers and bitter mothers and children in whom the flame of creativity burns white-hot.

In his long introduction to the 1965 edition that

brought *The Man Who Loved Children* back to readers' attention, Randall Jarrell claims that disappointment in the critical reception of the book in which Stead had laid bare her deepest pain and wounded compassion had diminished her genius from that point forward:

> When the world rejects, and then forgets, a writer's most profound and imaginative book, he may unconsciously work in a more limited way in the books that follow it: this has happened, I believe, to Christina Stead. The world's incomprehension has robbed it, for twenty-five years, of *The Man Who Loved Children*; has robbed it, forever, of what could have come after *The Man Who Loved Children*.[4]

Though I've read some of Stead's other works, I'm not an expert on them. Still, I'm not convinced that Jarrell's right. In the cutthroat world of publishing (far more cutthroat now than in Stead's time), more than one danger lurks. Those of us who hang on by our fingernails, who tore our own guts out writing and then publishing a book that contained the very best of us, only to find the reception lukewarm or cold, may have less to lose with the next one and more reason to make it sing louder, higher, deeper, more blazing. I'm speaking here of hardcore writers, not of people who find their niche publishing a series of mysteries or beach reads.

Either way—striking publishing gold or never knowing if this pile of words will win a contract—I suspect we write by believing in our potential, or we'd stop. What's your best book? people ask me, and I always want to tell them it's the one I'm working on now, the one that hasn't fallen to critics' judgment. And yet I cannot name a prolific author whose best book was her last book. Maybe we realize our potential the way Wordsworth crosses the Alps in "The Prelude," finding himself on the far side before he could realize he'd reached the pinnacle.

I'll have more on this topic toward the end of this study. Here, it's just worth observing that if Stead realized *The Man Who Loved Children* was her pinnacle, she didn't pause to gape at or mourn it. She had three other novels in mind; as she wrote to her stepmother, "I hope I get some backbone and go at it a bit faster than usual, for time draws on and I have only turned out *four* books."[5] But she had certainly dissected both her own past and the poignant origin story of a writer and daughter more ruthlessly than she ever would again.

MEN ON *THE MAN*

When so few readers know of a book and even fewer have written love letters to it, a fan is reluctant to quibble with a fellow fan. I am grateful to both Randall Jarrell and Jonathan Franzen for bringing the world's attention, even fleetingly, to *The Man Who Loved Children*. At the same time, I find some of their responses to the book remarkably at odds with anything I think Stead is doing, and equally at odds with what I most admire and wish I could emulate of her achievement.

Let's start with Jarrell, the award-winning poet and critic who brought *The Man Who Loved Children* back to the public eye in 1965, after it had lain dormant for most of the preceding quarter-century. In his lengthy introduction to the new edition, Jarrell characterized Stead's achievement: "If all mankind had been reared in orphan asylums for a thousand years, it could learn to have families again by reading *The Man Who Loved Children*." That claim makes me shudder, as does Jarrell's observation that "Sam is one of those providential larger-than-life-size creations, like Falstaff, whom we wonder and laugh at and can't get enough of."[6]

Jarrell loved the book and conveys plenty of truth about it, some of which I'll mention. But the family that *The Man Who Loved Children* could teach us to have would be a living nightmare, and I have never, in all my readings of the book, laughed at Sam, any more than I could be provoked to laugh at Hitler. When I close the book I have had more than enough of Sam Pollit, thank you very much.

The celebrated novelist Jonathan Franzen, writing almost a half-century later in the *New York Times*, makes a similar claim, writing of the "psychological violence" of the book, "And worse yet, you can never stop laughing at that violence." Of Sam, he claims, "There isn't a more hilarious narcissist in all of literature." Of the marriage of Sam and Henny, "What saves their hatred from being monstrous—makes it comic instead—is its very extremity." Of the book as a whole, "In a lesser work, this might all read like a grim, abstract feminist parable, but Stead has already devoted most of the book to making the Pollits specific and real and *funny*, and to establishing them as capable of saying and doing just about anything."[7]

Have I lost my sense of humor? I laugh at Falstaff; I laugh at any number of Faulkner's monstrous cartoons; I even found moments in *Crime and Punishment* that were hilarious. I have laughed at some of Henny's lines, because the snarky Henny, like many for whom humor is the only available coping mechanism, knows how to be funny. But my enjoyment of *The Man Who Loved Children* has nothing whatever to do with the comicality of its main antagonist.

At the risk of guessing the author's intent, I conjecture that Stead doesn't mean Sam to be funny. Yes, he's an idiot. His condescending, "enlightened" racism while serving abroad is cringeworthy. He says and does things that he means to be amusing, and sometimes he gets a laugh from one of his oppressed children. But his clownishness is a thin guise. How do we laugh at a man who sets his children violently upon one another? Who calls his supposedly beloved elder daughter "a mass of blubber," "fathead," "great fat lump," "mule," "full of hate," "a mean gutter rat"? Who humiliates his sensitive son by engulfing him in the slop of a boiled marlin? Who advocates for "murder of the unfit, incurable, and insane" and of "children born mentally deficient or diseased"? Who defends an incestuous father and excoriates his pregnant eleven-year-old daughter? Who brutally rapes his wife?

Sorry, guys. Maybe there's a joke. But I am not laughing.

A small matter: Jarrell refers throughout his forty-one-page introduction to the author of *The Man Who Loved Children* as "Christina Stead." Male authors he mentions include Tolstoy, Johnson, and Dostoevsky, none of whom requires a first name. When I served for a short time on a local community board, the board's minutes recorded what was moved or discussed by Mr. Smith, Mr. Jones, Mr. Zimmerman, and Lucy. Jarrell doesn't go that far, but my sense is that he couldn't bring himself to write simply "Stead." The standalone last name was too masculine; it would have placed Randall Jarrell in the same ancillary position he held vis-à-vis those male writers, rather than granting him the privilege of reminding us, with each mention of the author's name, that she was a woman.

Why am I nitpicking? Because with no other novel do I have the overwhelming feeling that I am reading this book as a woman; that as with some of those ambiguous images that make the rounds of the internet, I can see the picture both ways but commit myself to my perspective. Male critics like Jarrell and Franzen dismiss the details that constitute what I think is the "real" picture because those details (e.g., marital rape) aren't salient to those who read the book as a man. For a recent real-world echo of this sort of gendered perspective, glance back at the Brett Kavanaugh Supreme Court confirmation hearings. Is it the beer that matters? The operatic fury? Or that girl in her swimsuit, pinned down and thinking she might die?

Notice, too, how other ways of assessing this novel get cut off at the knees by Franzen's observation: "In a lesser work, this might all read like a grim, abstract feminist parable." No, he's not claiming that all feminist works are parables, or that all feminist parables are grim and abstract. But the catch is locked into place. If you find *The Man Who Loved Children* teaches you something stupefying about sex and power that you hadn't learned elsewhere, you are characterizing Stead's masterpiece as a "lesser work."

I was reminded by Franzen's essay of how large my own father looms in my relationship to *The Man Who Loved Children*. Franzen writes:

I suspect that one reason "The Man Who Loved Children" remains exiled from the canon is that Christina Stead's ambition was to write not "like a woman" but "like a man": her allegiances are too dubious for the feminists, and she's not *enough* like a man for everybody else. . . . Stead wasn't content to make a separate peace for herself, in a room of her own. She was competitive like a son, not a daughter, and she needed to go back, in her best novel, to her life's primal scenes and beat her eloquent father at his own game.[8]

In the 1960s, my mother had read up on the psychological literature, wherein adolescent girls were meant to rebel against their mothers and align themselves with their fathers. It alarmed her that I was doing the opposite (thus acting, in Franzen's words, "like a son"), so she packed my father and me off to a psychiatrist. At my fourth session with this kind man, he advised me that my best recourse was to leave home as soon as I was able. Was I responding to my father "like a son"? Or like his daughter?

Unwinding Franzen's analysis, we find, first, the

supposition that writers who write "like a woman" have "allegiances," presumably to the female characters in their books, and that writers who write "like a man" have some vague standard that Stead is unable to meet in the eyes of everyone besides feminists (who are also, in this reading, uniquely female and suspicious of Stead). Second, we find that, had Stead been writing like a woman, she would have occupied some private literary domain separate from the male literary domain. It's worth noting that Franzen twists the meanings of both "separate peace" and "room of her own" here to make his point. The first phrase refers most obviously to the John Knowles novel in which characters find peace in their own lives and not with the war; it's also a military term for the peace established between Country A and Country B even when Country A's allies remain at war with Country B. Here, though, "separate peace" implies that Stead's writing like a woman would mean accepting a restricted literary world for herself even while her so-called feminist sisters do battle. As for "room of her own," it's a remarkable sleight of hand to take Virginia Woolf's famous dictum—that to succeed as a female writer one must have money and a room of one's own— and transform it into a metaphorical room in which one remains, as a female writer, contentedly at home.

I'm spending so much time on Franzen's summary because it goes to the heart of both what Stead was doing and why her book has mattered enormously to me as a writer and a woman. Being competitive with one's father, even wanting to beat him at his own game (if that's what Stead was doing) does not define a child as a son or a wannabe son. If a father brings his competitive power and might to bear upon a daughter, then as a daughter—as a woman—she will push back. This is true in families, and it is true in the patriarchy that constitutes Western culture writ large.

What unites Jarrell and Franzen in their admiration of *The Man Who Loved Children* is the intersection of their characterization of the novel itself and their characterization of its author. As Franzen writes, "It's about a family"; or according to Jarrell, it "makes you a part of one family's immediate existence as no other book quite does." Women, of course, have written about families for eons. And I don't mean to deny that Stead's book centers on a family. But the domestication, as it were, of Stead's subject goes hand in hand with these critics' desexing of its origins. For Franzen, Stead aims to write "like a man." Jarrell, as I mentioned above, reminds us of the author's female status by repeating her first name. And yet his understanding of both Louie and her stepmother, Henny, removes from them the particularity of their position as females—one fully grown, one adolescent—in a very male-dominated world. For instance, writing that "the book's center of gravity, of tragic weight, is Henny," Jarrell views her tragic end as caused not by the desperate pass that her culture and her marriage to Sam have brought her to, but by "her character itself."[9] As for Louie, she remains for Jarrell a "little girl," thus eliding in his lengthy introduction the multiple ways in which her budding womanhood and Sam's sexual insinuations, sexual "teachings," and so on threaten to trap her in a perversely male spider's web of sexual domination. From Jarrell's and Franzen's laudatory reviews of *The Man Who Loved Children*, I get the sense that the family novel they love best is the family novel written by a man, or a woman writing in a manly way: the sort of novel written by, say, Jonathan Franzen.

Other male critics have found the novel astonishing not because it focuses on a family, but because, in their view, Stead is basically using the family structure as a way to launch a Marxist critique of society. When the novel reappeared in 1965, Jose Yglesias wrote in *The Nation*: "That this life [the life of 'an enlightened middle-class family'] is a fraud, that the family is a soul-destroying monster, that rejection and revolt is the only positive response, is always at the center of Stead's story."[10] And Australian critic Michael Ackland, writing more recently, reorients the novel to make Sam, not Louie, the "protagonist," albeit an ironic one, "an opportunistic appropriator [and] calculating manipulator . . . devoid of critical self-awareness, devoid of any genuine sense of social or racial justice."[11] These critics touch obliquely on one of Stead's greatest gifts to me as a writer, the constant presence of those pressures that the "domestic novel" purportedly sidesteps: money, class, the political barring of too many pathways to happiness.

Yet both these men, like Franzen, are careful to distinguish Stead's work from "the feminist modernist canon" (whatever that is), or "the merely personal" narrative that any woman who was not Stead might have concocted. Rather than raising the family novel to the status of a great work of literature because of its Falstaffian humor or its unwomanly author, they claim it as an ideological novel dressed up as a family story.

Female critics have generally taken views that, while equally admiring of Stead's greatness, recast the issue of gender and assess the character of Sam Pollit very differently from critics like Jarrell and Franzen. They also view a very real, not symbolic family setting as consonant with the novel's political implications. Angela Carter, for instance, in a 1982 review, clarifies the writing-as-X question:

> Although [Stead] has always written from a profound consciousness of what it is to be a woman, she writes, as they say, "like a man": that is, she betrays none of the collusive charm which is supposedly a mark of the feminine genius . . . She writes *as* a woman, not *like* a woman.[12]

Carter doesn't find the novel or its characters funny; she's more interested in "the single-minded intensity of its evocation of domestic terror." As for that room that Franzen envisions Stead eschewing, Carter observes that "'home' in Stead is almost always the patriarchal cage"— and one need hardly be a Marxist, or writing "like a man," to want out of that.

Jane Smiley—who should know, having written her Pulitzer Prize-winning family novel, *A Thousand Acres*, as a contemporary take on *King Lear*—understands how

The Man Who Loved Children works as a political novel *because* it is about family:

> What is at stake in the Pollit household is power, and Samuel Pollit is an absolutist who desires not only to invade his children's every thought, but also to have all their love and devotion. Big Brother in Orwell's *Nineteen Eighty-Four* is no more totalitarian than Sam Pollit.... Stead clearly understands that the family is not sentimentally walled off from politics, but is the source of all political feeling and understanding.[13]

Smiley notes how, "in a normal novel," Sam would be "a comic blowhard," like the Falstaff Jarrell aligns him with. Instead, she points out, *The Man Who Loved Children* is no "normal" novel, rather a work that attains "the grandeur of tragedy." She compares it not to Henry IV but to Medea.

None of the critics I've mentioned focus on the two aspects of Sam Pollit's character that are, for me, punches to the gut: his Nazified, racist eugenics, and his utter misogyny. Elsewhere I've read that whereas women will often complain about men they've known, men will tend to paint women with a broad brush. This formula holds true for Sam and Henny, as it did for my own parents. Henny is described as "one of those women who secretly sympathize with all women against all men," but her actual complaints are very specific—they're aimed savagely at Sam, "the Great I-Am," and secondarily at her bourgeois lover. By contrast, Sam waxes eloquent, to Louie no less, on the foibles of the so-called weaker sex: "Women have been brought up much like slaves, that is, to lie"; "Men call it the tyranny of tears, it is an iron tyranny—no man could be so cruel, so devilish, as a woman"; "Wimmin is prone to murder." Sam prefers baby girls to school-age girls, and school-age girls to grown women. This isn't a new trait in male characters, but what takes my breath away is that we understand this woman-hater from the vantage point of his daughter as she grows into womanhood. The choice of point of view, as novelist David Lodge puts it, "is perhaps the most important decision the novelist has to make."[14] When I first read about Sam Pollit from Louie's perspective, a door seemed to blow open, beyond which lay a vast, scarcely touched land of character and action on which I might now allow myself to tread. How is it, for us daughters who love fathers who hate women, to become, ourselves, women?

Sam's lethal eugenics are likewise gasp-inducing. Especially as I reread and taught the book, that aspect—evident in Sam's logorrheic addresses to his kids and also in his benevolent-white-man swing through Malaysia—felt as though it unlocked a key to my own family story, as I'll describe later in detail. In Sam Pollit, Stead doesn't put a domestic drama to the service of a Marxist ideology. (To a graduate student attempting to follow in Yglesias's footsteps, she wrote wearily: "No, I did not mean Sam to represent, i.e. be symbolic of, the US Govt. He is a man."[15]) Rather, she brings Nazism home—to America, to the family, to the systemic bigotry we still can't wrap our minds around today. That she has Sam mouthing lines like the following in 1940 gives me a chill:

"The extinction of one life, when many are threatened, or when future generations might suffer—wouldn't you, even you, think that a fine thing? Why, we might murder thousands—not indiscriminately as in war now—but picking out the unfit and putting them painlessly into the lethal chamber. This alone would benefit mankind by clearing the way for a eugenic race."

But I suspect that the final stroke in the novel that has me parting ways with its male admirers is Sam's rape of Henny. To get to that moment, I want to back up and say more about point of view. The Australian novelist Michelle de Kretser has observed, quite rightly, that what horrifies most about *The Man Who Loved Children* is the perspective Stead adopts, whereby the lethal dysfunction of Sam and Henny's marriage is seen from the point of view of the most helpless characters in the book, the children. Many critics have called the book's long tirades and dramas excessive, but as Kretser notes, "We find something excessive when it touches on our deepest emotions or fears,"[16] and among those are our memories of a childhood in which we were powerless to change a dynamic that threatened us. For this very reason, I find myself paying close attention in the few sections where children are *absent*—where we see Sam from Henny's point of view, or see the adult world through Sam's blinkered perspective, as in the Malaysia chapters. I've had the same sense of the world shifting when I've gone through my late father's diary and letters. The tricks that adults use on children don't usually work on other adults, so they adopt other strategies, or they reveal themselves more nakedly.

When we first witness a scene between Sam and Henny from Sam's point of view, we can feel him struggling to work things out with her and also struggling against his own conceit and arrogance. Henny, too, acts like a grown woman capable of generosity when she implores her husband, "Sam, let us separate! You're not happy. I'll go back to Mother and take the children while you're away, and when you come back we can fix things up without anyone knowing particularly." And when Sam wants to draw the argument to a close by having sex, Henny goes along, even knowing she'll likely become pregnant, because "to her alone this potent breadwinner owed his money, name, and fidelity . . . [and] his long fidelity to her, of which she felt sure, moved her beyond all her resolutions."

Toward the end of the book, the scene is very different—and we know how different it is, though we witness it from Louie's point of view, because we have been with these two adults as they hash out their doomed relationship. We've also been with Sam as he's looked at other women, especially younger women; we know full well he has a sexual appetite that's tightly bound with his sense of power. Once again, they're arguing, and now we know how Sam likes to close down the fight with sex; we even suspect that the fight itself rouses him. Louie, who's been listening in fear that her parents will kill each other, finally hears this:

> Henny gave a fretful hysterical laugh. "Oh leave me alone, you make me sick," and there was again a violent struggle, and then she heard Sam groan. . . . Louie stood at the door of Henny's room for a while with her heart beating fast, and heard Henny weeping.

It's the beginning of the end for Henny. Worse, when Sam encounters Louie the next morning, he happily passes off his wife's anguish as "the psychological storms and passions which poor Henny goes through."

I can easily imagine a male critic arguing that Stead hasn't given us clear evidence of rape; or that with a marriage this violent, how can you distinguish what's rape and what isn't? But both that earlier, transactional scene and Henny's emotional plummet following Sam's "groan" point directly to rape. Here is no jokester, Stead is telling us; here is no mere buffoon with his head in the clouds. This man is a killer. The next morning, he calls to his sons in his "crisp, gay voice." But when Henny emerges, the first thing she does is to beat her favorite child, Ernie, savagely, before she leaves for her sister's house and throws herself unsuccessfully at her insouciant lover. When she returns, days later, she passes Sam "with a black look, but a distant pasty one not like her old recriminatory ones." From that moment on, her thoughts are entirely with her children and their future; it's as if Henny, even before she commits suicide, has already erased herself from the scene. After hundreds of pages in which the arguments between two fundamentally incompatible people have gone on and on, the rape signals an extraordinary change. Once it happens, I'm reading a completely different book from the one that Stead's major male critics have read.

Sam's rape of Henny also throws into relief a point that Michelle de Kretser makes: that while our sympathy lies with Louie, the greater victim of Sam's tyranny will be his younger daughter Evie, who is "a feminine archetype: a beautiful, submissive little girl," whom Sam "regularly invites into his bed."[17] Shortly before he rapes his wife, Sam sets about defending the father in their neighborhood who has been charged with impregnating his eleven-year-old daughter. The next day, Evie tells Louie, "Daddy said I could be his wife." Sam isn't a pedophile; that would be too easy. Instead, he's a man who weaponizes whatever he can find—language, class, race, physical strength, sex—to maintain his power. There is nothing particularly Marxist or "man-like" about how Stead has constructed Sam's monstrousness; neither should observing that she has constructed it as a woman or a daughter or (yes, even) a feminist diminish the ferocity of the shift she induces in the book and the reader. It's a tour de force.

"What's at stake?" is the primary question a writer gets asked, or asks herself. In *The Man Who Loved Children*, the answer is: everything. That is, every hope for every character (other than Sam) hinges on Sam's megalomania and brutal sexism.

The only way to spring this fateful trap, in Louie's world, is through alternative levers of power—a mother figure (but the hopeless Henny kills herself), a neighboring mentor (but the neighbors use Louie to kill their cat), other relatives (who can't afford Louie), or agents of welfare, like teachers (but Miss Aiden falls short). In other words, Louie's only way to foil the trap is to leave it and the world which contains it behind. The siblings she leaves at Spa House are like the ones left behind in Omelas, in Ursula LeGuin's famous story, "The Ones Who Walk Away from Omelas." Meant to describe those with an unbending moral conscience, LeGuin's final lines apply equally to a certain kind of woman artist. It does the one who leaves no good to think about those who stay; we have enough on our plate. "Each alone, they go west or north, towards the mountains," LeGuin writes. "They go on. They leave Omelas, they walk ahead into the darkness, and they do not come back." Or as Stead writes of Louie, "She walked on. . . . As for going back to Spa House, she never even thought of it. Spa House was on the other side of the bridge."

MY FATHER, WHO
SOMETIMES LOVED
CHILDREN

In most ways, my father was Sam Pollit's opposite. Franklin Ferriss was born into a family of privilege. He attended private secondary schools, Yale University, and Columbia University before he returned home to St. Louis to take his law degree at Washington University. He was physically fearful and socially awkward as a young man, with weak eyesight and tendencies toward hypochondria and self-doubt. He went through a spell of agnosticism, but by the time I was coming of age, he was a devout Episcopalian.

Yet I was a budding artist and a dreamer, like Louie, and found my father to be a bully, a misogynist, a racist, and a hypocrite, much like Sam. Like Henny, my mother was a small woman, often bitter and furious with my father, with a penchant for Henny's kind of eating—curries, nuts, Scotch. (At one point my sister-in-law dubbed her the world's oldest living anorexic.) My father, by contrast, ate enormous quantities of food without gaining weight and liked to end dinner with a plaintive, "What's for dessert, Ann? No dessert? Not even Jell-O?" which reminds me forcefully of Sam's wheedling Henny for bananas: "I don't ask for much. I work to make the Home Beautiful for one and all, and I don't even get bananas. Everybody knows I like bananas."

Much has been made of Stead's having initially set the book in early twentieth-century Australia, with the Sam character based on her own father, David Stead. But she published it as a contemporary novel in 1940, when Sam Pollit is meant to be in his mid-thirties. Born in 1911, Franklin Ferriss was of roughly the same generation as Sam. A tall, fit, somewhat ascetic-looking man, he remained acutely aware of the ways he fell short of a masculine ideal that governed his ordering of the world. In 1934 he began keeping a journal, in the tradition of his father and grandfather. He wrote in a flowing Palmer script with carefully structured sentences, addenda, even footnotes. Unlike his ancestors, who recorded important national events, the births of children, and the deaths of elders, my father was introspective and devoted most of his entries to self-examination. Now, he was not, like Sam

Pollit, a monster. But there are aspects of his diary entries that clue me in to how my dad acquired his difficult personality, why he reacted to me as his daughter the way he did, and why I respond so strongly to *The Man Who Loved Children.*

In his diary, my father is prone to sweeping theoretical pronouncements balanced against expressions of his own desires and shortcomings; he has little interest in other people, places, or situations as they present themselves to him. A recurring theme emerges first in his reflections on his dismal social life at Yale: "The problem was that I had a full dose of that peculiar Ferriss mixture of pride, lack of self-confidence, and indifference, when I was born; and that I had only gone partway in overcoming these traits when I went to Yale." These "traits," as he sees them, are inherent in his bloodline, which he also defines purely as a male bloodline. He refers to such qualities frequently, always as something to "overcome" that remains immutable.

Equally immutable in the diary is one's place in the caste system. My father's main problem when he's finally drafted into the Army (having failed to sign up because "I did not want to run the risk of losing my life to keep Germany from being top dog in Europe") is finding "congenial" male friends. (With women he is less particular: "a strong masculine interest in girls made me less demanding in the way of personality and intelligence than I was with boys.") He denies being "snobbish" but claims of most men he meets as an Army private, "what interested them didn't interest me"—which proves an insurmountable barrier to friendship, since he views his own interests as hardwired. He eventually breaks up with the one woman he's seriously interested in because "her background and personality gave her quite inadequate equipment for the social life of St. Louis"—this from a man whose own social skills, by his admission, have failed to develop, and who feels socially inferior to his classmates at Yale. From my girlhood, what I most recall is my dad's barking at us to lock the doors when we were in the car at a red light and a Black man was crossing the street. "I don't know what's wrong with being a servant," he used to say. "If I had been born into the servant class, I would have been happy to be a servant."

For many years, and intensively during the five years after he returned from military service in Europe, my father wanted above all to "get married." He wasn't particularly in love with anyone ("I don't have the girl lined up, unfortunately"), but he ran through a long list of women—whom he calls "girls" even when they're in their thirties—and found all of them wanting. In one case he notes there is something wrong with the girl's mouth. In another, she "has too many old-maid habits." In yet another, he decries "the immaturity of her looks." Still another "is the mental superior of most boys," not a desirable trait. His common complaint of his own "social ineptitude" suggests that he wants an "outgoing" wife who will make up for what he laments as his own failures (and social success is the real success he wants), which meanwhile derive from his fixed views on "congeniality" ("I have made no efforts to make friends where I felt no congeniality"). He has little positive to say about the women in his family, either. His sister Ruth is "vain," his mother is "unbusinesslike." When he finally meets his future wife on a lunch date, she has to leave to teach a class while he dawdles to talk with someone, and for months he holds off from contact because he is "shocked at her rudeness" in leaving so abruptly.

By this time, my father was thirty-nine, living in his parents' home, on the cusp of permanent bachelor status. When he discusses his various doubts about my mother—her age, her public-school education, the difference between their social groups—his father finally instructs him: "Franklin, marry her. If it doesn't work out, there's always divorce."

Like Sam Pollit, my father preferred babies to girls, and girls to woman. He initially liked me because I struck him as a "feminine" baby. When he was dating, he liked the younger "crop of debutantes" even as he recognized he'd aged out of their cohort. A chasm seems to exist, in both my dad's and Sam's worlds, between men and women, and the preference they each occasionally express for women seems wholly derived from desire or the enjoyment of a power they notably lack among men.

Despite his degrees from Yale and Columbia, my father was also like Sam Pollit in his anti-intellectualism. Though he writes, "I never had any real trouble with my studies," he professes no interest in the content of what he learns:

> I just jammed them into my head, knowing it was my "duty" to get good marks and instinctively wanting to do reasonably well what was manifestly my job. The same factors were responsible for my years of violin practicing ... [I] never thought to wonder if I was honestly enjoying it.

Later, he concludes, "I have a deep lack of confidence in the academicians' thinking about economic problems," and his increasing bias turns to narcissism:

> On most of the great issues that have aroused man's curiosity, I am really only interested in what I think about them. . . . The truth is—and I believe it is my own misfortune—that I have no deep interest in the fine arts. . . . The analysis of my own problems and their solution was the part that I really enjoyed. I enjoyed it because I used to spend a whole lot of time thinking about those problems. . . . The goal in life is to obtain the greatest amount of happiness possible during life. If truth is not necessary to a man's happiness, let truth go by the boards.

Again and again, my father returns to two main problems—that he doesn't find one or another field of endeavor sufficiently interesting, and that he falls short in his social relationships with other men. Like Sam, what he wants is to be important, and to be recognized as important. He does not really long for friends—that is, he hardly complains of being lonely, or of liking someone who fails to reciprocate. Rather, he identifies social success as necessary to the project of being important in the world, and for that reason he simultaneously detests its transactional nature and wishes he could succeed in it. Ironically, the war work he never signed up for proves later to have been a rare high point. On returning to law practice in 1947, my father writes:

Two main factors seem to be unsettling me: 1) the lack of social significance of my daily legal work, against the background of national and international problems of the upmost [sic] gravity; 2) my lack of natural aptitude for practical politics and for the related techniques of building a law practice. Re (1)—My job as liaison officer between M.I.S. and the State dept. in '43 and '44 impressed me with the satisfaction to be had in work that is directly related to the solution of significant national problems. Re (2)—While I have made considerable improvement since high school days, I am not by nature a good mixer—partly on account of indifference to so many people. . . . Such a personality trait is a real handicap to building up a good law practice and is almost a fatal defect to being successful in practical politics.

Unlike my dad, Sam Pollit is incapable of introspection. In the few moments where we see him alone, as on his jaunt to Malaysia, he is either bothered by the heat or waxing both nostalgic and horny:

> Dressing in fresh linens, he felt with pleasure a cool, wet wind blow; relief was rain and the eternal wet blanket of the night air, but it was relief. He let it blow away his thoughts of the distant past. . . . He felt as if the ghost of his own mastered desires, potency that had sunk into the earth, had grown up, a genie that was surrounding him, seizing him, thrusting him out of his honest path into the flame-leafed tropic jungle of desire.

Absent of psychological insight as he is, Sam feels himself at the mercy of qualities over which he has no control and a fate that "seizes" him, transforming his memories of his late wife to a "jungle of desire." That same fatalism, tied to eugenics, "unsettled" my father and gave his "traits" the power, as he saw it, to work their will over his every time.

Sam Pollit and Franklin Ferriss are also characters caught at a certain moment in history—Sam in the novel, my father in his diaries. Much of their anxiety centers on white masculinity and their role as white men. Like so many in the Great Depression, my grandfather Henry Ferriss saw his fortunes plummet, from being the president of the Investment Bankers' Association to finding himself unable to pay for his son's law school education. White masculinity felt under threat generally during the 1930s, with relatively more female employment and male dependence; significantly, white men would take jobs perceived as "Negro work" but not those perceived as "women's work."[18] Birth rates declined. Roosevelt's New Deal public murals tried to "remasculinize" America by showing hard male bodies at work.

As I grew curious about the resemblances between Sam and my father, I started to see them both as creatures of their time. Sam is soft, ill at ease in the working world of men. Throughout the novel, his status as a provider falls. He shores himself up by constantly placing himself above "wimmin"—"En if I had my way no crazy shemales would so much as git the vote! Becaze why? Becaze they is crazy! Becaze they know nuffin!" My father's constant worry about a suitable profession hinges on what is appropriate for him to do and what will land with enough masculine force to overcome his social and physical ineptitude. Having begun, as a young man, with no sense that his choice of profession depended upon its earning potential, he found his marriage foundering largely on his inability to maintain our household in the style that his own upbringing—and my mother's ambitions—had led them both to expect. With his disastrous marlin enterprise, Sam Pollit resorts to entrepreneurship, a recourse touted in the 1930s to solve chronic unemployment. My father turns to what he called "the bug of self-improvement," another feature of 1930s masculinity.

Almost every instance of cruelty or rigidity can be chalked up to these men's tentative hold on their male position. For instance, when his sons Ernest and Saul start fighting, Sam eggs them on—"Good hit!" "Take it like a man, you fathead," etc.—and justifies himself after with "When there is bad blood in the family, I want you to get it out of your system by a man-to-man fight." On my son Luke's thirteenth birthday, my father sent him a long letter describing the fight he'd had with a "bully" at school and encouraging Luke to use his fists. The incident finds an echo in his diary:

> It would have been better perhaps if I had had even more pride, for then I might have gotten into more fights and started earlier on the long battle to overcome my instinctive physical fearfulness. I was even afraid of my two older playmates, Bill and Bing, particularly the latter, tho' I remember fighting each of them at least once and "cleaning up" on Bill.

A sense of threatened masculinity attends the episodes where Sam humiliates his children—Louie by filching her diary and forcing her to read it aloud; Ernie by taking his meager savings and distributing them among the others; and most notably Little-Sam, who vomits from the stench and grease of the marlin:

> He took Little-Sam by the neck, drew him out of the washhouse, and, when he stood on the newly cemented yard outside the door, suddenly flung the liquid over him, drenching him. . . .

Sam did not even laugh but considered his son triumphantly. Not a tremor passed over the boy's face. He stood dripping with the juice, fish tatters on his head, one long shred of skin hanging down over one eye.

My father, too, humiliated his children; in fact, I cannot remember his laughing except at those moments, and even then I felt there was anger lurking behind the chuckles. The diary hints at causes. Of his own father, Henry, he writes, "I do believe it is a fact that Father, though quite sensitive himself, is at times insensitive of, or just careless with, others' feelings." Of his younger sister Ruth he writes of incestuous "games" they played as children until "our consciences got the better of our natural desires," and after that point he brags, "I could make her cry within two minutes any time I wanted to."

That hint of incest attends *The Man Who Loved Children* both in Sam's insistence on his "partnership" with Louie and especially in his treatment of Evie, the "Little Womey" that Stead has symbolically named after the first Eve. Sam promises—or threatens—that he will have to make Evie his wife because Henny is out all day. Evie whispers the news to Louie confidentially at first "not sure whether she would laugh or approve." But later, when the children overhear Sam accusing Henny of having given birth to another man's child, Evie bursts into uncontrollable sobs, as if to signal the terrible fate that awaits her when her mother leaves.

In my own family, my younger sister was the Little Womey character—the "sweetest of my children," in my father's diary. He thought her docile and pretty, unlike me. Often he mistakenly called me by his sister's name, Ruth. At my sister's wedding, he drank too much and, plopping down next to me, leaned over and asked, "When are you going to get a pair of woman's bubs, girl?" And yet I have a vivid recollection of the night my parents argued bitterly and my father passed through the bathroom that connected their room to mine. Wordlessly, in the dark, he tucked himself into my twin bed and spooned me. There was nothing more—no erection, no sexual touching. For a long while I controlled my breathing, until finally I fell asleep. In the morning he was gone. Like Sam, he seemed a man who longed for a child to be his wife, so that he might be enough of a man to be up to the challenge.

To read *The Man Who Loved Children* is also to be reminded of views that hindsight renders horrific but that were not uncommon in the United States when Stead was penning her novel and my father his journal. Eugenics was pervasive at the time in rich industrial societies, including countries like Canada and Sweden that we now think of as beacons of decency. Oliver Wendell Holmes's majority Supreme Court decision in *Buck v. Bell* (1927)—"It is better for the world if, instead of waiting to execute degenerate offspring for crime, or to let them starve for their imbecility, society can prevent those who are manifestly unfit from continuing their kind"[19]—was not out of the mainstream, though it sounds to us today like Nazi propaganda. Sam Pollit simply takes Holmes a step further:

> Murder of the unfit, incurable, and insane should be permitted. Children born mentally deficient or diseased should be murdered, and none of these murders would really be a crime, for the community was benefited, and the good of the whole was the aim of all.

My father never advocated extermination of "the unfit," nor did he advocate sterilization except in bemoaning the high birth rates of "colored races." He did assign his psychological traits to "Ferriss genes," and noted their emergence in my brother at a young age. He understood "Negroes" to have been born with lesser intellect than "whites." In 1939, he didn't consider it worth breaking from his nascent career to save a degenerate Europe. When my mother wanted a fourth child, he said he would allow it only if she could guarantee a boy. Genes, gender, bloodline: these were the gold or tin coins of life.

Daughters of these men, especially daughters with ambition, occupy a precarious position. Our roles are pre-assigned. Our roles are impossible. If we are not to be doomed to domesticity, like Evie, we have to fight, and sometimes to fight ugly. Louie can wither her father's pretensions with a sharp line. When Sam ponders aloud whether to name his "system" of human perfection Monoman or Manunity, she coolly replies, "You mean monomania." When, after working for five years, my mother spent her savings on a family trip to Europe, I was thirteen and entering what felt like full-on warfare with my dad. In Salzburg, my mother sent us to a room to hash out our differences. "You didn't even pay for this trip," I said to my dad. "Mom did."

"I contributed a thousand dollars," he said.

A thousand dollars sounded like a fortune to me. Still

I curled my lip and retorted, "That's peanuts." Satisfied that my hit had landed, I watched his face crumple. Out of grace or pride, he did not mention that none of my mother's earnings went toward supporting our family; his did.

Before I look at what it means to be the evolving woman artist fathered by a Sam Pollit or a Franklin Ferriss, I want to pause on Henny. I feel such profound sympathy for her, and I so admire Stead's ability to conjure such a character that I want always to push back against the critics who deem her a hysteric, a hag, a spoiled Daddy's girl who loves her own tirades. That Henny is not Louie's biological mother is both the point and beside the point. It is the point because the true movement of the novel takes place between these two women, with Henny unloading all her invective on Louie at the beginning and collaborating with her in the end. It is beside the point because the tension for Louie centers on her supposed resemblance to Sam and difference from Henny—a resemblance and difference that shapes a child and an artist even in families bound by biology.

My mother was of middling height and an hourglass figure, with thick wavy hair and an impeccable sense of style. She'd had a hard childhood but was wildly popular, witty, a smoker and drinker, full of moxie. I was tall, gawky, my hair thin and drab, my clothes always ill-fitting and just off the mark. Dreamy and sensitive, I had trouble making friends and burst regularly into tears. For these reasons among others, I was quickly viewed as "taking after" my dad. At the same time, I knew there was an essential, unbridgeable enmity between my parents, an enmity that seemed the hatred of men for women and vice versa—and being on my way to womanhood, I wanted to side with my kind. Just as Louie watches Henny conserving her small, exotic meals, I watched my mother spread chutney on crackers and make candy of our discarded orange peels. When I think of how she looked, very late one night when I surprised her in the dark kitchen as she was quietly consuming the can of Eagle Brand Condensed Milk that she had boiled into caramel, I feel I could easily have been Louie, shapeless in a flannel nightgown, coming upon the dark, sharp-nosed Henny in one of her secret rituals. Like Henny's grownup jingles, which Stead contrasts with Sam's baby talk, my mother had a store of mordant, clever bits of wordplay that we loved to hear her recite. Here's Henny:

I would not marry a butcher, I'll tell you the

reason why;

He'd chop me up for mincemeat and put me in a pie.

And here's Ann Ferriss:

One bright day in the middle of the night, two dead boys came out to fight.

Back to back they faced each other, drew their swords and shot each other.

The deaf policeman heard the noise, came and shot the two dead boys.

Many readers have not been fond of Henny. Stead makes liking her difficult because above all she doesn't want us pitying her. It's surprising, then, to reread the novel and discover Henny's virtues. Despite her grousing about Sam's relatives, when the family holds a party to welcome Sam back from Malaysia, Henny contributes "little iced cakes with chocolate tears upon them [and] raspberry wheels." At the end of her love affair with the opportunistic, callow Bert, she faces the situation candidly. Comparing how impressed she once was by his "jumbo BVDs" to the emptiness of his "moral BVDs," she confesses that she needed her lover's help. "And you," she tells Bert frankly, "weren't there."

Though the unemployed Sam excoriates Henny for wasting money, we see her selling her family jewelry to buy clothes for the children, including—especially—Louie. While Sam pins the debts she leaves after her death on her spoiled profligacy, all we know of her spending is that she needs clothes and food for their family.

Most important, in every situation that involves disempowered children and powerful parents, Henny takes the side of the children. When Sam's sister, Jo, arrives to complain that their sister Bonnie has shown up with a baby that Jo has had "taken away," Henny explodes: "Where is the baby? . . . Where is the baby, Samuel? What is it, a girl? A boy?" and calls the uncaring Jo a "big, brass-mouthed old-maid cow." When Sam orders the children to take turns day and night watching the cauldron in which he is boiling the marlin into oil, Henny dismisses them and stays up all night watching and stirring the reeking pot. Being a mother actually suits Henny; it is being Sam's wife that horrifies and degrades her.

In all these details I find glimpses of my mother— even though, as with Sam and my dad, I look at their social class and movement between classes through different ends of the telescope. Henny is the "spoiled daughter" of David Collyer. She admits herself that her background has failed to fit her for the tough life she needs to live. Ann Hennigan Ferriss, my mother, caught tuberculosis from her Irish immigrant father; at nine years old, she was in the hospital when she learned of his death. As the daughter of a demanding widow who never remarried, she grew up comfortably, but with a sense of being disenfranchised. Her steady college beau was killed in World War II; to marry the working-class man she next fell in love with, she would have been required by contract to give up her job at IBM; and so, at age twenty-nine, she settled for my father and "married up." Like Henny, she resented what she considered our poverty, and like Henny she protected her softer sentiments with a rough exterior.

Here's the core of what that awful term "relatability" refers to. When an author like Stead creates characters so real we can practically smell them, we find those aspects of our lives that seem, somehow, to be like theirs, regardless of how unlike we are in all other aspects. Stead hasn't taught me *how* to pull this off, but she shows me that it's possible—because look! Here they are.

NO WONDER THEY ALL
LAUGH AT ME

How many *Künstlerromanen* feature female protagonists? *Little Women* comes to mind. *The Song of the Lark*, by Willa Cather, fits the bill, though it's not her best book. Virginia Woolf's *To the Lighthouse*, published shortly before Stead began writing *The Man Who Loved Children*, features an artist coming to realizations about her art, but the character of Lily Briscoe doesn't dominate the novel the way Louie does *The Man Who Loved Children*. In other words, if I went looking for narratives of girls developing into writers or artists just as I was developing into one (and I'm sure I did look, at least subconsciously), the pickings were slim. That they were surely even slimmer for Christina Stead makes her creation of Louisa Pollit all the more remarkable.

Though Louie knows quite clearly that she is the offspring, not of sharp and bitter Henny but of the dead saint, Rachel, she never gives her biological mother much mind. She is far more invested in winning the approval of Henny, who seems to despise her. "Boiled owl," "sullen beast," "stuffed pig," "creeper," she labels Louie. At the same time, Henny buys her a new dress when she has almost no money. When she sees the effect of marital strife on Louie, she gives her two inherited Dresden figures that Louie has craved, saying, "It is a rotten shame, when I think that the poor kid is dragged into all our messes." Sam insists that Louie is just like him, that they are bound together by blood and the memory of her mother—and as a result, the last thing Louie wants is to be like her father. Again and again she refutes him, finally coming to the entry he finds her making in her journal while he yammers on—*Shut up, shut up, shut up, shut up, shut up, I can't stand your gassing, oh, what a windbag, what will shut you up, shut up, shut up.*

Yet when it comes to art—to poetry and playwriting—Louie lays all her gifts at her father's feet for him to trample. Finding her diary, written in code, he makes her read it aloud and humiliates her. When she organizes the children to perform her play "Tragedy: the Snake-Man," written in her own invented language, Sam waxes furious. With all his purported love for humankind, nature, etc.,

Sam has no use for art or creativity. That realm, if it exists at all in the Pollit household, belongs to Henny, who crochets and tufts coverlets and mattresses, who recites witty doggerel, who makes clever desserts.

"Tragedy: the Snake-Man" is actually a coded account of Sam's tyranny over his daughter—and yet neither Sam nor Louie seems to recognize its autobiographical source or pointed intent. Louie writes it in an invented language with traces of Latin, e.g. "As mother says, I am rotten" emerges as "Cumu mat dic, ia cada." The father in the play fails to understand that he is the snake strangling his daughter, and that his embrace kills her. Louie's siblings try to perform the play, and when Evie can't remember her lines (given that the language makes no sense to her), Louie steps in to speak the part of the daughter.

"Why isn't it in English?" Sam keeps asking as the play stumbles along. The first answer, I suspect, is that creative children like to make up their own language. I know I did. I spoke to my cat in it. I puzzled over its grammar. The Biblical Adam got to name all the flora and fauna of Paradise; I wanted that same power. The language I grew up with seemed already to have been commanded and regulated by the adults, but when I talked to the cat, I reigned over my world. We don't know if Louie follows the same impulse. She answers her father's question with "Did Euripides write in English?" and when he presses her further, she presents him with a vocabulary list and the precise English translation of the play. Rather than praise her inventiveness, he says, "Blow me down, if I know what's the matter with you. Instead of getting better, you are getting more and more silly. . . . If Euripides or any other Dago playwright makes you as crazy as that, you'd better shut up your books and come home and look after your brothers and sister."

The remarks cut; Louie has a major meltdown and shuts herself in her room. But the invented language and Sam's reaction to it have effectively diverted him— and maybe the reader—from the biting despair of a play whose central line is "Fear to be a father and be hated by your daughter."

Novelists talk a good game about showing and not telling, about being in a partnership with the reader whose apprehension of the text is what creates meaning. But go looking for examples of writers following their own advice, and you'll find yourself led by the hand most of the time. It was tempting for me as a young writer to drop hints here and there, to be sure the reader at least understood why I was including this or that scene or line of dialogue. But Stead sets down the whole of Louisa's incomprehensible play, followed by the whole of its translation. She includes no scene where we are inside Louisa's head, understanding the motivation behind either the language or the play. We then get Sam's reaction and Louie's humiliation. Full stop. Stead takes the risk of leaving Louie's "Tragedy" entirely in our hands.

A *Künstlerroman*, like a *Bildungsroman*, is a coming-of-age story and so dwells on adolescence, which means focusing on the discomfort of a changing body and the extravagance of romance. *The Man Who Loved Children* is an outlier only in its insistence on Louie's physical hideousness and the literary manifestations of her love. I was the opposite of Louie, physically, but ugliness visits both ends of the spectrum. In fact, I'll conjecture that becoming a writer or artist is more difficult for beautiful adolescents: they spend less time alone and have less occasion to make common cause with the old, the odd, the outliers.

Both Henny and Sam call Louie names. She is a beast, a fathead, a mountain of fat, a miserable sulky wretch, an obstinate cuss, a mulish donkey, a dogged wretch, a mass of blubber; her writing is called sickening tommyrot, stupid, silly, nauseating stuff. Now and then her wall of desperate faith in her own genius cracks, and she cries out:

> "I am so miserable and poor and rotten and so vile and melodramatic, I don't know what to do. I don't know what to do. I can't bear the daily misery. I can't bear the horror of everyday life... . No wonder they all laugh at me. . . . My elbows are out and I have no shoes and I'm so big and fat and it'll always be the same. I can't help it."

I once participated in a panel discussion of creative writing professors concerned about the fabled workshop, the core of the creative writing curriculum that has defined a universe of MFA programs. Their students, they complained, seemed not to interact well. They were all too timid, too aloof, or too loud; they needed better social skills. I demurred. I suspected that most of us had become writers in part because we were socially inept. I didn't see the point, if better writing was what we after, in making everyone socially ept.

This did not go over well, but I still think it's the truth. I recall my own adolescence as a series of humiliations.

Where Louisa was too big, I was too skinny. I was a year younger than the others in my all-girl class. Even when I developed breasts they were small, and my hips remained narrow. I was too weak and clumsy for any of the sports teams. Often Louie is reminded how much she resembles her father physically ("yellow as light honey"), and the physical likeness implies a character likeness that horrifies her. In my case, I had my biological mother as an ideal. Released from a childhood spent in a tuberculosis sanitarium, she had enjoyed her adolescence immensely, surrounded by friends and laughing her way through high school. My father was the tall, skinny one. He was also the perpetually absent-minded one, the tardy one, the one who declaimed at supper and would not be interrupted, the sanctimonious one. Of these traits I wanted no part. Yet I was a daydreamer, a storyteller, a moralist, and a girl lost in her own head. Socially I was at least as maladroit as my father had pictured himself in his diary. I needed to keep my feet on the ground, adults told me. Every time I floated away from the solid structure of daily obligations, I knew I was acting like my selfish and despised father. To this day I want to rip my head off whenever I lose something or arrive late.

At the same time, Louie and I both long for our

father's acceptance. There are moments, certainly, when that acceptance seems to arrive without straining or risk. Louie likes to walk in the dark, and Sam walks with her. My father and I were the hikers in our family, summiting the soft peaks of the Ozarks after canoeing its rivers. Louie and Sam play word games. My father and I danced—fox trot, waltz, to the melodies of Cole Porter and Straus, my small feet atop his black Oxfords. So I don't mean to suggest that these father-daughter relationships are all antagonism and abuse. Rather, the ways these men try to mold their intense, dreamy daughters become more startling in the context of what feels like reciprocal love. I think, for instance, of the piano lessons I was forced to take. Why my father chose me, of his three children, to learn the piano, I will never know. I had no musical gift. For some years I had a teacher, a bitter chain smoker who owned three large cats and was the pianist for the St. Louis Symphony (as my father never failed to remind me). I took my lessons at her house, where allergies clogged my sinuses and made my eyes run; I couldn't tell, sometimes, whether I was crying or having a reaction to the cats and smoke. My father sometimes attended these sessions, where he sat silent in a dark corner of the teacher's living room. Feeling his disapproval of every wrong note, I grew to hate the piano and never became more than a mediocre pianist. And yet I didn't give up, because I wanted his love.

Only in my sixties, reading his diary, did I understand that my father hated the violin he was made to practice throughout his childhood. Today, almost two decades after his death, I still play on the same instrument I practiced so phlegmatically decades ago, and I find joy in the touch of the keys—joy I think my father, whose violin sat untouched on the top of a tall hutch in our dining room, never got to experience. Stead, late in life, described herself as a scientist, trained in the method by her father and glad to apply it in her fictional characterizations.

Like Louie, I hungered for the genius I felt certain lay buried inside me. In summer camp—where, as in school, I was a year younger than everyone else—I somehow auditioned successfully for the part of Pish-Tush in the camp's production of Gilbert and Sullivan's *The Mikado*. When the counselor directing the musical realized that I couldn't sing, he initially had me speak my part, then he replaced me. I thought this was how the world worked.

I couldn't stop writing, performing, inventing, even when I thought, like Louie, "No wonder they all laugh at me." I gave my sixth-grade music teacher a carefully scrawled score of my song "April Showers Bring May Flowers," four verses and a jolly refrain, and she taught it to the class, and they laughed at me. In drama class, when we were preparing a short play about the building of the St. Louis Arch, I was caught reading a book, and as punishment I was assigned to write a contribution to the play. Throw me in the briar patch! I wrote a poem addressing the Arch (as "thou"), whose verses all began "O Arch! My Arch!" To general titters and my deep shame, it was included in the play. I heard the whole school, laughing at me.

Like Louie I was messy, melodramatic, "vile." My parents didn't call me names, but neither did they encourage my odd pursuit of writing; I puzzled them. The sensitive girls in books with whom I was meant to identify—girls like Scout in *To Kill a Mockingbird*, who like me was a tomboy with no desire to mature into a "lady"—moved from ugly duckling to swan through their innate compassion and love. They became happy. They became wise. They didn't become writers.

Maybe it's possible to become an artist without a keen interest in death. I have not done a deep dive into the history of the *Künstlerroman*, but I suspect that the protagonist in most examples of the genre, like the eponymous hero in *The Sorrows of Young Werther*, encounters and dwells on mortality more often than his (or, rarely, her) companions.

As an adolescent, I was obsessed with death. In a series of dreams that extended over several years, I faced various imminent deaths (by fire, by falling, by drowning, by the sword) and escaped them only by willing myself to shut my eyes and wake up. In another recurring dream, something enormous was coming at me too fast for me to escape; my mother considered this an ether dream, but to me it felt like a mortal encounter with the sublime. Christian notions of death—angels, etc.—held no charm for me. I spent several months in a swoon over Keats, who died young and unaware that his art would live on, despite "Ode on a Grecian Urn." "Here lies one," I repeated softly to myself sometimes, in bed at night, "whose name was writ in water." My early poems and stories were morbid, centering on children doomed by cancer; on the moment a deer becomes aware of the hunter; on the image with which my mother had endowed me, of herself as a tubercular child sleeping on the roof of the Chicago children's hospital covered by ten blankets and an inch of winter snow, next to the boy she liked who died.

Death also hovered over the stories I embraced: Andersen's "Little Match Girl," who lights all her matches to see the image of her grandmother and is found stiff and cold on New Year's morning; the *Narnia* tales, with the noble death of Aslam; *At the Back of the North Wind*, where the boy Diamond is finally found, "white and almost as clear as alabaster." I read *Charlotte's Web* thirteen times, each time knowing that Charlotte would die and wanting to see it through.

The Man Who Loved Children is haunted by death, and Louie in particular cannot escape it except in those moments when her "senses reel with love." She sets her own conditions in the first part of the novel: "'If I did not know I was a genius, I would die: why live?'" She also commits an act, early in the narrative, that both presages her role as a murderer and shows the length to which she follows her curiosity about death. She frequents the house of their neighbors, the Kydds, a childless couple who have "a strange vileness in them and in the house which fitted their solitary lives perfectly." One day, the unctuous Mrs. Kydd asks her to perform a task that she can't manage herself: to kill her cat. Louie readily agrees, though when she goes to pick it up, "she felt a fear of the mad beast, and a wicked lust to drown it and finish it, just because with all its shrieking it was helpless." When Mrs. Kydd has filled a bathtub,

> Louie got the box and pushed it under. The cat struggled with large floating gestures in its prison. At the first convulsion Louie felt a sort of sickness, then she pushed it hard under and, sitting on the edge of the bath, kept it under with her feet. The box heaved a little. The cat took a long time to drown.

I could never write a scene like this one. I would be too fearful of making my protagonist "unlikable." When I first read the book, I thought Stead had committed a grave error in shaping Louie's hideous side so early in the book, so we can never forget it regardless of how deeply we may sympathize with her later. My students, when we discussed Louie, recoiled at her in this moment and couldn't understand why an author would include it. But I return again and again to the scene. It affects how I view Louie for the rest of the book. By the end, it feels like a dress rehearsal for her attempt to murder both her parents—until she finds that killing people you love is too big a leap from killing a neighbor's cat. I notice, too, how we get no access to Louie's inner thoughts from the moment of that "wicked lust" to her leaving the cottage, when "she was sorry that she had only been invited over for the cat." That mental detachment, the allusion to her horror only as a physical sense of sickness—it's all part of the ruthless job of being an artist, standing in the scene and yet apart from the scene, writing it down. Or as James Joyce would have it, "refined out of existence, indifferent, paring his fingernails."

Sam, of course, views death as a cleansing mechanism, a way to rid the world of all weaker beings, including those whose weakness lies in being unattractive. ("But you would keep yourself alive," Louie mordantly reminds him.) Henny and her mother and sister, meanwhile, gossip about death with a sort of delight. Henny's monologue is practically a Molly Bloom soliloquy of suicide. She lists permanganate (a poisonously acidic disinfectant), drowning, gas, nitrous oxide, carbolic acid, arsenic, and cyanide, among other methods, only to dismiss them as too unpleasant. She could swallow two hundred aspirins, she suggests wryly, "but my heart would kill me," and while opening a vein in a warm bath sounds nice, "I think I'd be too weak. Why be in misery at the last?"

Henny will take cyanide in the end, but the point of

her lighthearted, morbid conversation with the women in her family is that death is always there, familiar, beckoning. Even the young, in *The Man Who Loved Children*, are tempted by it. Louie's desperately poor friend, Clare, ties the cord of a Venetian blind around her neck and "accidentally" falls out a window. When Ernie sacrifices all his money to his doomed mother, he makes and hangs an effigy of himself. Death is the open door, the one sure escape from a life without redemption.

Death's antidote is art. *Ars longa; vita brevis.* Like most who begin writing fiction at a young age, I simply wanted more words. Rosellen Brown captures this early urge in her essay "Don't Just Sit There: Writing as a Polymorphous Perverse Pleasure": "As a child I wrote for comfort, for invisible power, for the astonished pleasure of the *feel* of the letters . . . . This was a time of polymorphous perverse pleasure in language, with no end outside the moment, no end outside myself."[20] It didn't take long, though, for the fact of my own mortality to impress itself upon me and for me to put my hope for everlasting life into my sentences. And so I felt myself on the fulcrum of a seesaw, a fulcrum that in Stead's work is sharp and high as the peak of the glass mountain: On the one hand, I could not write about life without facing death head on; on the other, I had to believe in my artistic immortality to make the writing worthwhile.

In first grade, on pages folded together into a book, I created a set of stories based on a boy I knew and disliked, a six-year-old bully down the block who had been diagnosed with Type 1 diabetes and would have to give himself daily injections of insulin or he would die. This news turned the boy, for me, from a crewcut pest into a wounded hero, and I sent him on all sorts of adventures in which, seconds from death, he finds his insulin and manages to jab it into his thigh.

My first published story, accepted for the school lit mag when I was in seventh grade, concerned a girl whose negligent parents are exiting the house for a party while she watches on TV the news of the Six-Day War in the Middle East. She's got one of those hollow rubber dolls in her lap, and as the front door shuts and the television closes in on clips of howitzers, she takes the doll's head in her hands and with her thumbs pushes its face in. Neglect a child, my little story said, and you make her a killer. When we were first allowed to take a creative writing class in high school, I received permission to skip a half-dozen homework exercises to write a much longer story, which concerned a girl who'd fallen down a well and was slowly perishing while the world went on unaware of her plight.

I have no idea what I intended with these stories except that I saw no point in writing something that failed to grapple with danger and death, however little I'd seen of either in my own life. The stories I read and wrote urged the reader to love the one who died or who risked dying; death ennobled a young creature, made them precious, lifted up their lost potential.

This same romanticism drove me to seek a teacher, a mentor—any adult, really, who would single me out as special and love me for what I felt sure I could do. The only one who fit the bill came and left early: Miss Hope, my third-grade teacher, all of twenty-two when she took her first job at my elementary school. A shiny cap of brown hair encircled Miss Hope's round, acne-scarred face, and I thought her chic and lovely. She seemed to have nothing in common with the stiff-hipped, girdled women who had taken charge of earlier classes. Miss Hope had ideas. She listened to our ideas. We should publish a newspaper, I told her, and she smiled and nodded and said, "What a great idea," and before long I had corralled my classmates and strong-armed them into calling it the *Hope Digest*. I wrote most of the articles while others pasted in pictures. We ran the thing off every week on the school's mimeograph machine. The pages smelled delicious, like gasoline.

Years later, Miss Hope came to one of my readings. She had taught primary school for only a few years. The pay was awful, the demands exhausting, and when she'd had her fill of it she'd pivoted to a sales job at McDonnell Douglas. She was only thirteen years older than I was. She seemed mildly disappointed in her life, and the words I dug out to tell her how she had inspired mine felt hollow and insufficient. Still it thrilled me a little when she said she remembered me, that she had taken pride in me.

Louie's object of adoration, Miss Aiden, also comes and goes quickly. She actually enters the book as an object of mockery by Louie, who has found that her cheeky wit earns her admirers at her new school. When Louie concocts a hilarious tour de force of nonsensical wordplay in place of the day's lesson, Miss Aiden grins at the joke rather than punishing her. Louie's writerly heart and creative energies turn toward her teacher like a flower to the sun. Secretly, for Miss Aiden, Louie writes a crown of sonnets; eventually, she invites her to Spa House for dinner. The day itself is so packed with incident that it seems Miss Aiden's visit will have to supply some sort of catharsis. It begins with Sam's birthday celebration, where he scorns Louie's gift of her unintelligible, furious play. It continues with Ernie's discovery that Henny has sold all her jewelry and robbed his money box to keep them in clothes and food, while Sam cavorts with the neighborhood children after school. Meanwhile, Louie rushes around the house madly to make everything look as presentable as a thirteen-year-old girl can manage when the glassware is down to exactly one intact glass. By the time Miss Aiden arrives, we feel we've exhausted all the Pollitry that the book has to offer. Then Stead pulls a point of view switch:

> Louie had on the same soiled dress that she had worn to school, Miss Aiden observed, with hurt, for she had expected to be treated with more ceremony.

Here is Stead's point, and the whole point of including Miss Aiden. The outside world cannot be counted on to see who you really are or what situation you're in, because the people there have their own agendas, always. In Sam, Miss Aiden observes only "a lively, agreeable, unassuming man, with a lot of information that he was anxious to bestow upon her; he was very jokey too"; in contrast to Henny, whom Miss Aiden sees as "a black-eyed, feverishly rouged hag." She is appalled by the family's poverty and, like Sam, "saw truth, beauty, and progress in terms of the twenty-five cent story magazines." Finally, Stead captures Louie's heartbreaking disappointment in her idol with a subtlety at odds with the melodrama of the preceding action. We change back at this point, to Louie's perspective:

> "Your father is very amusing," said Miss Aiden, patronizingly. For the first time, Louie found the shadow of a ghost of a fault in Miss Aiden's manner.

Why do I adore this line? It's far from the catharsis the reader's anticipated. It leads to a dead end as far as Miss Aiden is concerned, because she exits the story, never to return. I think I adore it because in these two sentences we glimpse both Stead's authorial remove from her characters, a remove she never shies from using to the advantage of the story; and because when she turns her gaze, from that remove, on Louie, it aches with compassion. Miss Aiden is callow, self-serving. One day, Louie will remember her with clarity and know how unworthy she was of the sonnets, the play, the worship. But we're not there yet. We're only at the point where "the shadow of a ghost of a fault," a thing unseen, scarcely whispered, marks Miss Aiden in Louie's eyes. What sort of shadow can a ghost cast? And what is the fault? Not disliking Samuel Pollit, whom Louie both loves and hates; not succumbing to his charms. Rather, Miss Aiden diminishes both Louisa and her father—first, by assuming that Louie wants her father to seem amusing; and second, by reducing what we now understand as a family tragedy to a joke. Louie's love for her teacher— possibly for any teacher—has been dealt a feather-light, mortal blow.

For all his posturing about the higher callings of humankind, Sam Pollit is essentially a Philistine. Stead suggests his incuriosity and prejudice in lines like the one where he refers to Euripides as a "Dago playwright." And yet he gives the adolescent Louie the greatest gift a parent can give a budding writer: classic texts. His selection, to be sure, is both strange and designed to teach her about sex, and you suspect that if he has read these texts, he has at best misconstrued them. First up is Shelley's *Poems*, which are heavily Romantic and address a range of topics from unfettered nature to state revolutions, with a persistent refrain of death and decay and practically nothing to do with sexual relations. Sam would have bought such a book not for its contents but because it was written by an atheist who believed in free love and held radical political views. Little does he expect that Louie, swept up in Shelley's extravagant language, will fasten onto Shelley's verse drama, *The Cenci*, focused on a young woman who kills the tyrannical father who has raped her—and will recite parts of it back to Sam.

Next, Sam gives Louie *The Golden Bough*, by James George Frazer, for what he calls "the anthropological side of the question" of sexuality. Here again, the intent and the outcome are at laughable odds. Though Frazer considered himself an anthropologist and his volume on pagan beliefs influenced early anthropologists, his ideas as a social scientist were widely discredited by the 1920s. But Sam's attraction to *The Golden Bough* is easily discernible in the anthropologist Godfrey Leonhardt's later description of the book's fall from grace:

The central theme (or, as he thought, theory) of

The Golden Bough—that all mankind had evolved intellectually and psychologically from a superstitious belief in magicians, through a superstitious belief in priests and gods, to enlightened belief in scientists—had little or no relevance to the conduct of life in an Andamanese camp or a Melanesian village, and the whole, supposedly scientific, basis of Frazer's anthropology was seen as a misapplication of Darwin's theory of biological evolution to human history and psychology.[21]

Sam's entire attitude, on display particularly during his sojourn in Malaysia, accords with Frazer's debunked premise on the "scientific" evolution of (presumably white) "mankind" from supposedly primitive, superstitious beginnings. As anthropology, then, what he has given Louie is junk. As literature, though, it may be unparalleled. The mythic constructs running through the dense pages of *The Golden Bough* have influenced generations of writers from Yeats and William Carlos Williams to H.P. Lovecraft and Doris Lessing.

Finally, *The Bryce Report on German Atrocities in Belgium* that Sam bestows on Louie was a piece of British propaganda, published in 1915, that featured exaggerated, lurid accounts of Germans raping and pillaging their way through occupied Belgium. It feeds Louie's imagination in a rape-fantasy, bodice-buster way, "fill[ing] her daydreams and night thoughts with the mysteries of men's violence—women crucified . . . young girls sent into barns with detachments of soldiers and 'the ripening grain,' soldiers winding the hair of women round their sabers and thus dragging them to the floor to satisfy their bestial desires." That's the effect of Sam's gift. Its intent becomes clear only in the anecdote that immediately follows, in which a neighboring "roustabout" father stands accused of raping and impregnating his eleven-year-old daughter. To the reader's and Louie's horror, Sam is incensed, not by the crime, but by the judgment of "a father in his own home." In other words, what the father has done, like what the soldiers have supposedly done, like what Beatrice Cenci's father does in Shelley's drama, is *normal* to Sam; is to be understood under the same "scientific" lens as the conclusions of Darwin's *Origin of Species*, another text Sam bestows on Louie.

Everything about Sam's gift of these classic texts, then, misfires in terms of his own arrogant, misogynist and racist understanding of the world. Yet they hit the mark for a wildly imaginative young writer, who now understands that "under the eternal belching black organ pipes of Bethlehem Steel was the vile lake that covered an agony of fire, a lake that hid something like Grendel, or the pained bowels of an Aetna, or the cancer of a Prometheus."

I had even more access to classic texts than Louie, and like her, I obtained several of them from my father. The Pollit home has fallen from the fragile cliff of aristocracy on which Henny once rested; mine clung to the upper middle class most visibly by displaying my parents' books. Owning books was still a marker of social class in the 1950s. We had shelves of cloth-bound hardcovers in the living room and less elegant shelves of popular novels and reference books in our second-floor hallway. As my siblings and I grew into reading for ourselves, I worked my way through the elegant collection of world tales in the *My Book House* collection preserved from my father's childhood. Later I could pluck volumes of Dickens or Twain at random. I recall my father's stopping in the living room at one point when I was starting in on Jane Porter's 1809 "history," *The Scottish Chiefs*, 520 pages of romantic fantasy illustrated by N.C. Wyeth. "You're too young for that," he remarked, but he didn't take the book away. I immediately became determined to make my way through the whole bloody, majestic story of William Wallace. "Bright was the summer of 1296," the book began, and already I was in love with its syntax.

For all his book ownership and his Yale education, my father was, like Sam, a Philistine at heart. His love for Wordsworth and the King James Bible was more or less reflexive. In his diary he confessed his indifference to art, literature, and history. Instead, having "jammed" his academic studies into his head, "by senior year the bug of self-improvement, which has dominated me so long, showed up in my determinedly setting about to read all the famous novels extant. While my friends played basketball, I would retire to a parked car and force myself, for the most, thru 'Les Miserables,' etc." In later years he wondered aloud why he'd been compelled to read Boswell's *Life of Samuel Johnson*. He dutifully attended St. Louis Symphony performances and listened to radio broadcasts from the Metropolitan Opera on Saturday afternoons. For the most part, he slept through them.

Yet I grew up thinking of my father as the knowledgeable one, sensitive and cultured compared to my mother's hard, bright edges and love of comedy. In the end it was to my father's status-conscious collection of classical music that I owed my love of Beethoven and

Grieg, just as the books that otherwise gathered dust on our shelves sparked my imagination. It was in the ongoing attempt to win my father's love that I memorized Wordsworth; that for the seventh-grade diagramming club (yes, I was its president), I diagrammed Luke 2:29–32 ("Lord, now lettest thou thy servant depart in peace, according to thy word, for mine eyes have seen thy salvation, which thou has prepared before the face of all people, a light to lighten the Gentiles, and the glory of thy people Israel"). Hoping for his approval, I kept singing in the junior choir even when I started fainting in the hot robes and bright lights of the choir stalls. Hoping he would speak to me in the French he'd learned abroad during World War II, I took a high-school semester in Belgium and became fluent in the language.

My father found my singing voice grating. My French was arrogant. Why was my nose always in a book? If I had to write stories, couldn't I find a nobler subject— Moses, for instance, or Joan of Arc? It confused me, as it confuses Louie, that the gifts I laid at my father's feet were ignored or scorned. ("See where Looloo walks by herself, thinking her thoughts," says Sam with a grin to Louie's brothers. "Always thinking, always mooning.") Little did Louie or I know that these powerful men had never once fallen under the sway of the words, the texts, the musical notes we learned in order to gain their favor. Little did we know that by the time we came to rebel against the men, those words, those texts, and those notes would have us forever in their thrall.

MOTHERHOOD
AND READING

"Had she hugged her children instead of beating them," the critic Madeleine Schwartz has written, "the book might have become a feminist classic."[22] She's speaking of Henny, of course, and while I suspect that Henny hugged her children often enough (well, maybe not Louie), it's only the beatings we witness in *The Man Who Loved Children*. From that detail alone, I might have inferred that Christina Stead never had children herself, even if I hadn't known her history.

I have two children. I've never contemplated the idea that having children may have made me a lesser writer. If I've considered the question at all, I think I've concluded that motherhood has opened me up to varieties of human experience that I would otherwise have known only from the outside. At the same time, as my friend, the writer Jayne Anne Phillips, has observed, it's not just the time that children take from your writing life when you become a mother. They also, and more crucially, take your imagination. So much imagination goes into being a mother, especially when children are young, that left to yourself and the cursor blinking on your screen, you feel your own banality firing from every neuron. I remember a creeping, frustrating guilt emerging during a ten-year gap between books. It's only in looking back that I grant myself pardon for the years when I was working full-time, giving birth, scrambling for childcare, moving for better jobs and better schools, and making up bedtime stories every night. (Yes, every night. They had to feature trolls. The trolls had to have names. There were twenty-six trolls, whose adventures all took place after the humans had gone to bed. When I went away to a conference, I recorded nightly troll stories for my husband to play to the boys. I don't remember a single one of the plots.)

Becoming a mother—and continuing as a mother through single parenthood and a new partnership and challenges that persisted after my children became adults—has changed my reading of *The Man Who Loved Children*. I still identify with Louie; the book persuades the reader to identify with Louie. I still believe that Stead, with her insistence on fidelity to "real life," possesses the extraordinary imagination that James Joyce attributed to memory, that is, the ability to recall and connect the whole of an experience and cultural moment so that they spring to life on the page. It's not inconsistent with this belief to affirm our ability to create characters and lives we haven't inhabited. Hardy didn't have to be female to triumph with *Tess of the D'Urbervilles*; Hilary Mantel didn't have to change her sex or travel through time to create an unforgettable Thomas Cromwell. So I'm not saying that Stead couldn't create believable parents except by being a parent herself; she *does* create believable, albeit monstrous parents. What she does not give us is their subjective experience of being those parents. It's that subjective experience—or the absence of it, on the page—that I began to feel as I reread the book after my sons were born. I want to be clear about this: Becoming a mother hasn't lessened my reading of *The Man Who Loved Children* or my admiration for Stead. It has changed it, though.

Throughout her life, when she was asked about the characters of Henny and Sam Pollit, Stead responded in one of two ways. She often acknowledged frankly that they were modeled on her own father and stepmother, and she was especially pleased when Thistle, David Stead's third wife, confirmed the likeness of Sam to David. At other times she answered in more psychological terms. She wrote several letters to a graduate student inclined toward a symbolic analysis of her work, including the presentation of Sam as the eternal child:

> Of course, Sam is a child—he was the youngest of his family. A member of a family tends to retain his position, throughout life; the youngest remains the engaging, dependent youngest, however clever; the eldest remains the eldest, unable to bear patronage, being independent, not caring to join societies—for *he* is the head forever. . . . But I must tell you that when I was writing *TMWLC,* I saw on the back of a political pamphlet of my husband's, the title "Paternalism in the Family" (or something near) and I thought to myself, "Yes, that is what my book is about."[23]

What's curious about Stead's response, here, is that as a reader I feel that the paternalism she mentions should be Sam's. But from her characterization of Sam as a typical youngest child, it seems she's talking about him as a son, not as a father.

This makes sense to me, but a different kind of sense than it would have made if I had read her letters in the 1980s, before I had kids. Then, absorbing *The Man Who Loved Children*, I understood the oppressive politics of the Pollit family as Louie came to understand them— as, I think, Stead understood them. Henny and Sam, Henny especially, were a miserably married couple. As parents, Henny struggled and failed while Sam wreaked lifelong damage on his children. How they experienced parenthood didn't enter into the equation. Not because we never entered their point of view; we are in Sam's head while he is in Malaysia and at several other points when he engages with Henny or his sister Jo, and we get Henny's view of both Sam and her lover, Bert. But they don't think about their children at any of those times. As parents, they exist only as the children, especially Louie, perceive them.

Before I became a mother, it didn't occur to me that anything was missing in this full-throated family portrait. And I'm not sure anything *is* missing. The book doesn't ask us to consider how Sam feels as a father, whether he worries more about one child than another, whether he lies awake at night rehearsing something curious from the kids' horseplay that afternoon. It doesn't ask if Henny enjoys nursing her baby or finds it to be one demand too many of her body that the children pull at and crawl on and wrap themselves around. The difference for me, now, is that I bring this particular curiosity to the book and find myself discovering that, subjectively speaking, Henny and Sam don't exist as people who are parents.

Stead remained ambivalent about becoming a mother all through her childbearing years. Pregnant in 1934, when she was writing feverishly, she had an abortion. Later she experienced at least two miscarriages. To her friend Florence James, she wrote of children, "I do not yearn for them: my ideas have turned to other channels."[24] She claimed that her husband was the one talking of children, though later in life she would say that he was the one who never wanted them. She described her own loneliness as "maternal."

Plenty of other women writers have shared this ambivalence. One, a close friend when we both had our first child, was adamant that she wouldn't have a second child until she had signed her first book contract. Alice Walker thought you could be a mother and a successful writer if you had a child, "but only one."[25] When the writer Lauren Sandler expanded on this idea, she got pushback from a clutch of writers who had borne more than one child.[26] The novelist Lily King staked out the other side of the argument: "Once I had kids, my sense of self was no longer completely defined by my success or failure as a writer. It's given me confidence as a writer to try things, and worry less about failing."[27] But so long as we live in a world where motherhood presents a larger practical and emotional burden for women—and certainly that was Stead's world—ambivalence seems reasonable, and the choice to forgo children doesn't strike me as limiting.

What I'm saying, instead, is that now that I've immersed myself about as deeply as one can in the experience of parenting, I could not write a book like *The Man Who Loved Children*. Part of me would want to dwell for a time in Henny's state of mind, not as wife or sister or lover, but as a parent. And while Henny's *role* as a parent matters to the book, and her stance toward her children may be inferred from her actions, her subjective *feelings* as a parent remain absent. My being a mother, then, messes with the ways this book affects me as a writer. There's a fork in the path: I go one way, Stead another.

Mothers have featured, or at least have been considered *qua* mothers, in much of my own fiction of the last quarter-century. I want to explore ways their stories shatter the conventions about how mothers should feel toward their offspring. I'm aware that relatively few novels highlight the point of view of mothers, or perhaps of parents in general. Though motherhood itself, especially working motherhood, is no more commonplace than any other way of experiencing life, it seems to risk tedium. I remember the shock of Sue Miller's *The Good Mother*, with its robustly sexual divorced mother, appearing in 1986. Anne Tyler's mothers, perhaps because Tyler herself is a genius at domestic life, have managed to have their say. Other novels of mothers often show them in extremis— negotiating the psychotic rapist imprisoning mother and child in Emma Donoghue's *Room*, contemplating suicide in Michael Cunningham's *The Hours*, killing the child before she is taken into slavery in Toni Morrison's *Beloved*.

Even if Stead had borne children, one could argue that in *The Man Who Loved Children* she is relying on her own childhood, her own experience of having a father and stepmother. Even when we become mothers our-selves, we don't necessarily take up the perspective of the generation that mothered us. And yet I do, more and more. It's that tendency in myself that I'm keenly aware of, as I reread *The Man Who Loved Children* these days.

I'm curious as to how my mother felt about having kids; I'm curious about my grandmother, giving birth for the first time in 1919 at the age of thirty-eight.

Part of me feels there's a sort of purity lost as a result of the perspective I've gained. *The Man Who Loved Children* is pure in its view of the family and family relationships. Its surface is roiled, for sure—by the awful, interminable, frenzied fighting; by Louie's lurching from one project to another; by the grinding reality of the family's fall into poverty—but the gaze remains directed from child to parent, from parent to adult world. I've stepped slowly away from the person I was when I first read the book. It's as if, looking at a painting or photo of the magnificent front of a house, I've always known that the house has four sides, but now that I've been on its back side, I've seen those porch steps, the weedy back pathway, the herb garden. I look at the painting and still find it extraordinary, but I can't get those other unpainted, unseen, unimagined things out of my head.

WRITING TO EXCESS

TOO MANY NOTES

One reason I was drawn to novels, as a young reader and writer, was because they were imperfect. The Great American Novel, like the Great Novel of anywhere, was by definition an unattainable ideal. The form was newer than poetry, playwriting, the short tale, or the essay. It hadn't had time to develop the notion of perfection. The very name of the form suggested constant newness, the form inventing itself and failing to fulfill itself at every try. As an enthusiastic but sloppy thinker, I thought I had a chance here.

What was more, novels could be imperfect, seriously flawed even, and still achieve greatness. At the local public library of my childhood, below the police station and next to the fire station, the librarians finally answered my pleas to be allowed to check out novels from the adult section by permitting me to enter the stacks behind the circulation desk and read there, so long as I was sure to replace the books where I had found them on the shelves and not to tell anyone where I had been. At Louisa's age, I sat on the concrete floor under the hanging lightbulb and over the course of several weeks read the novels that would have bookended the books by Lucy Ferriss, had there been any. The first was *Rebecca*, by Daphne DuMaurier, which I loved for the storm-drenched scene that reveals Rebecca's sunken ship and decomposed body. The second was F. Scott Fitzgerald's *Tender Is the Night*, where I failed to understand what the fuss was all about but I loved lines like "Somewhere inside me there'll always be the person I am to-night." I knew these novels had flaws, though I was too absorbed by the words to tell what those flaws were. Meanwhile, from the bookshelves in our house, I was working my way through most of Dickens, Stowe, Tolstoy, and Austen, and all of Thomas Hardy.

A decade later, my master's program required us to take oral examinations in two pre- and two post-1900 writers, one each of fiction and poetry. My fiction choices were Eudora Welty, who wrote mostly short stories, and Hardy. I loved Hardy's characters, especially his women—Bathsheba Everdene with her passion for the land, Tess with her refusal to play the victim, even *Jude the Obscure*'s abstemious Sue. But there was never any doubt in my mind that Hardy's novels could write themselves into corners (the convenient suicide of Jude and Sue's three children), take long and meandering byways (Clym's studies in *The Return of the Native*), and introduce characters undeserving of the space they took up (Lucetta Templeman in *Mayor of Casterbridge*). The plots often creaked, as did many of Dickens's and Tolstoy's massive constructions. That their greatness overcame their glaring defects gave me hope. Maybe you didn't have to solve every narrative problem to produce great literature. Maybe literature shattered the frozen sea within us not just despite its faults—the inconsistent characters, the languors, the irresolutions—but because of them. As the poet Richard Howard put it, when a friend complained of finding a classic book boring, "Yes, that's one sign of a great work. It has long, boring stretches."

The chief complaint, over the decades, about *The Man Who Loved Children* has been its excess. Randall Jarrell makes the charge:

> The weakness is, I think, a kind of natural excess and lack of discrimination: she is most likely to

go wrong by not seeing when to stop or what to leave out.... A few things in *The Man Who Loved Children* ought not to be there, and a few other things ought not to be there in such quantities.[28]

I'm reminded of the scene in the film *Amadeus* where Emperor Joseph II praises Mozart's work with the caveat that there are "simply too many notes," and Mozart replies that there are just as many notes as the piece requires.

I'm also reminded of the famous description of Yonville l'Abbaye, the forlorn provincial village where Charles Bovary takes his passionate, voracious wife in Flaubert's *Madame Bovary*. For years I handed students the three-page description of Yonville without directing them toward a particular reading of it. The comments I received were unintentionally hilarious. Dutifully albeit painfully, the students tried to praise the extensiveness and specificity of the writing and to close with a points-earning opinion of "this is great literature." In class, when I pressed just a little, they admitted that they were bored past tears with Flaubert's description; they had fidgeted in their seats and wanted to smoke a joint or light their hair on fire, anything to escape the monotony of phrases like our first introduction to the area around Yonville:

Before us, on the verge of the horizon, lie the oaks of the forest of Argueil, with the steeps of the Saint-Jean hills scarred from top to bottom with red irregular lines; they are rain tracks, and these brick-tones standing out in narrow streaks against the grey color of the mountain are due to the quantity of iron springs that flow beyond in the neighboring country.[29]

"Now," I would tell the students when they had been allowed to vent their spleens against the passage they had so brown-nosingly praised, "you have some idea how Emma Bovary felt."

I think of Flaubert as a high-wire walker, taking his risks without a safety net. Young writers are always being encouraged to show and not tell. But how to show the reader how deadly boring, how screamingly banal, how crazy-making dull is Yonville l'Abbaye without stultifying the reader? The question matters, because if we aren't thoroughly vexed by the tediousness of the place, we won't sympathize with Emma's rash and eventually suicidally reckless behavior—and if we don't sympathize with Emma, it's game over for the rich, humane irony of *Madame Bovary*. On the other hand, a bored reader quickly becomes a nonreader, and that's game over as well. Thus, the wire. Just as many notes as the piece requires, no matter what the Emperor thinks.

Foreshadowed by her willingness to drown an innocent cat, Louie's attempt to murder her parents forms the climax of *The Man Who Loved Children*. If this plot turn seems only a species of *grand guignol*, we'll hold the book's author accountable and assign the book to a corner reserved for peculiar, unrealistic, bloody farces. For Stead's novel, like Flaubert's, to achieve pathos, the author can't just tell or even show us how horrifying are the circumstances of that home and the narcissism of its patriarch. She has to immerse us in it until, as Jarrell rightly points out, "it will take you many years to get the sound of the Pollits out of your ears, the sight of the Pollits out of your eyes, the smell of the Pollits out of your nostrils."

It's hard to offer just a taste of what Jarrell means. Stead dramatizes five full-scale battles between Sam and Henny, three of which occupy several pages of vicious dialogue dripping with mutual contempt and designed to inflame. Sam has the advantage in physical strength and patriarchal standing, but when it comes to language Henny gives as good as she gets. He calls her "you devil of rust and rot and boring"; she dismisses his "rotten fine thoughts," accuses him of exploiting her father's influence, hurls her disgust at him: "You were breaking my bones and spirit and forcing your beastly love on me … while I hated and detested you and screamed in your ears to get away from me." Condemning the hateful vengeance of all women, Sam accuses Henny of whoring; she reviles his "dung-haired sister." Words like "vile," "rotten," "devilish," "misery," bear much repetition. Sam follows through on his promise to "shut you up," by backhanding his wife across the mouth.

Just as torrid fights between Sam and Henny recur throughout the book, so do scenes of abusive parenting. For instance, having lectured the children for two pages about a system of futuristic transport in which passengers would disintegrate and be carefully reassembled, Sam turns to Louie. In his utopia, he explains, she will tend to other women while Ernest runs the "Planned Economy." When Saul, one of the twins, objects that he "won't do what Ernie says," Sam "chuckled and winked at Louie" as he seizes the chance to set his sons on each other. He goads Saul into hurling insults, and then prods Ernest:

"Go on," whispered Sam, letting out a kick at

Ernest. . . . "Go on, Ernest-Paine!"

"I'll murder you for that," yelled Ernie at once. "I'll push in your daylights."

Sam flattened the grass with both hands and squatted down in a flat place, saying gleefully, "Go on, Sawbones, give it to him; go on, Ernest-Paine, attaboy!" . . . "Take it like a man, you fathead," cried Sam to Saul. "Fight him; what are you bawling for?"

It's almost physically painful to read this prose. No wonder editors and critics thought Stead should trim the drama, or reduce the number of examples of it.

And yet. Excess isn't excess, says Mozart—and Flaubert, and Stead—when it's a necessity. I realize that this motto sounds suspiciously like Barry Goldwater's "Extremism in the defense of liberty is no vice," but just as Marxism can produce bad governments and good literary criticism, so a dangerous political slogan can serve an undaunted literary project. Mozart asks the Emperor which few notes he would like the composer to take out. Reading *The Man Who Loved Children*, I find it is only at the point where the scenes become too excruciating to read that my imagination glimpses how harrowing they must have been to live through. I'm not confident that Stead could remove a single paragraph of Henny's ravings over the vileness of the world, or Sam's sanctimonious tyranny, without leaving behind a kernel of doubt as to whether the whole situation is bad enough for Louie to respond as she does. Consider the episode where Sam premasticates his sandwich and, calling over four-year-old Tommy, "To the boy's pouted lips he joined his own, siphoning the chewed sandwich into Tommy's mouth." The disgust quotient of that one moment is enough to turn away readers. But without it—without tasting Sam Pollit's saliva laced into a spongy blob of bread and meat in our own mouths—I'm not sure Stead could convince us of the impossibility of tolerating Sam. Ditto Henny's relentless, Medean misery, and Louisa's encoded literary extravaganzas.

I began this discussion praising the imperfection of novels, and I don't mean to say I think Stead's is perfect. To my mind, the self-indulgence others complain of surfaces in a short section detailing Louie's summer vacation with her dead mother's relatives, the Bakens, in Harpers Ferry, Virginia, where "there were no ghosts in the cupboard, for everything was told with Biblical simplicity." Yes, the summer gives Louie some surcease from her impossible

life, but in the end it doesn't matter. The Bakens end up
too poor to accommodate Louie; the visits end; and the
real story lies where it has always lain, in the savage house
of Sam and Henny Pollit. But even if the chapter is a
misstep, it simply puts Stead in the same category as all
the other novelists I've mentioned. I can be critical of
the summer-vacation tangent without diminishing the
greatness of what the novel achieves. Ditto, I want to say,
all novels.

For many years, my own early work made me cringe.
To be fair, my first four novels were published by major
New York City houses without any editorial intervention
beyond copyediting; the fifth, published by a university
press, fared likewise. I sometimes sat across the desk from
my editor at the time and chatted about publishing in
general, about the cover for my novel, the marketing
plans. The manuscript sat between us, often with little
yellow or blue flags sticking out from the pages. The
editors seemed embarrassed to speak about the story, as
if it were so strange or the characters so opaque that they
wouldn't admit of discussion. I would ask if we should talk
about whatever was written on the flags, but they would
wave a hand and say no, it doesn't matter, copyediting can

clean things up. I found myself wondering why they had bought my novel if they liked it so little.

Now, flipping through the pages of my first book, *Philip's Girl*, an autobiographical tell-all campus novel, I find the cringey moment: a short episode, narrated in retrospect, where the male professor's jealous daughter takes her baby sister out to the desert on a vague mission to alarm her father. She gets herself bit by a rattlesnake, but through some magical intuition, the professor drives out to the scene and saves her life. The whole thing is both melodramatic and underplayed, reduced to dialogue and summary. I remember wanting to use the landscape of Southern California more; I remember fearing that the emotions in the narrative would seem boring or silly if I actually dramatized them. Thus this truncated, incongruous scene. It's a bad moment in a young writer's novel, but it doesn't kill the work. The work itself no longer makes me cringe; it has solid moments, threads of original truth, and a few excellent sentences all bound between covers in the form that I already knew allowed for gaffes and soft spots. I don't think I had read *The Man Who Loved Children* while I was writing *Philip's Girl*, or I would have dared to write the actual scene rather than putting it to the service of some heartfelt aftermath. And then I would have risked the charge that's leveled at Christina Stead over her book: excess.

Once, at a writer's colony, I confessed over dinner that I was worried that the manuscript for my sixth novel was starting to top 450 pages. "Keep going," said a gangly, generous poet, "women should write long novels." When I pressed him to explain, he pointed out that men were always penning doorstoppers; in his view, so long as women continued to produce slim volumes, they wouldn't be taken as seriously. I don't know if he's right. I do know that beginning with that book, I faced editors who wanted to edit. And editing meant cutting, cutting, cutting. My writing changed—not in a bad way, necessarily, but in a way that cast a cold, practical eye on excess. If something had already been made clear in one scene, I would cut the scene in which it was made clear again, though differently. Dialogue would not go on ad nauseam. Narrators would curtail their pensiveness. If I wanted otherwise, I would have to fight for it. In today's publishing market, Stead would have a battle on her hands to preserve Henny's torrents of rage and Louie's desperate, peculiar play.

Recently, my fourth novel, *The Misconceiver*, one of the unedited ones, came to light again. I'd written it in 1997, when warnings were flashing across front pages predicting that the Supreme Court's decision in *Roe v. Wade* could soon be overturned. I set the novel in 2026, two decades after the imagined *Roe* overturn and fifteen years after the passage of a personhood amendment to the Constitution. When the book was rediscovered and a publisher wanted to bring it out of the remaindered shadows, I had no usable manuscript; the whole thing had been saved on floppy disks that time had corrupted beyond repair. So I scanned my last remaining copy of the book and set about, in the resulting document, correcting the millions of errors—*1* reading as *l*, *rn* reading as *m*, periods reading as commas, and everything vice versa. I proofread my own manuscript perhaps four times. Since the rights to the book had long since reverted to me, I could have chosen to change not only mistaken predictions of technology (e.g., we call them smartphones, not minilaps, and they don't need a wired connection), but also narrative errors, especially scenes or exposition that went on too long. One review a quarter-century ago, for instance, had criticized a late section of the book in which the first-person narrator, Phoebe, drifts away from civilization, stops eating, hallucinates, and almost dies. There was "little sense," one reviewer wrote, in the "confusion" of this section.

Reading through the manuscript—reading as if the book had been written by someone else, so long had it been since I'd written it—I disagreed with the reviewer. The core of the novel is Phoebe's inability to reconcile the twin pressures on her life—on one hand, the pressure of honoring the legacies of her mother and sister, both of whom died because they performed abortions; on the other hand, the pressure of the society in which she's grown up, which considers her a murderer. The events of the book conspire to bring both these pressures to a boiling point. In *2001: A Space Odyssey*, the central computer, HAL, goes mad when he can't resolve the conflict between his programming (which requires truth) and his orders for the mission (which require lies). *The Misconceiver* isn't interested in having Phoebe go mad, but it is interested in making the reader feel how impossible it becomes to go on living a life at odds with oneself. The section immerses you in Phoebe's own confusion and slippage, so that the means by which she recovers and forms the choice that ends the book makes sense. It's the high wire again, and if I'm going to walk it, I have to live with losing some reviewers.

SENTIMENTALITY

Not all excessive books earn their excess, nor do they

all suffer the editorial knife. Hanya Yanagihara's doorstoppers, *A Little Life* and its follow-up, *Paradise*, sink deep into their extravagant tales of abuse, sadism, exploitation, and psychic as well as physical crippling. Honorée Fannone Jeffers's *The Love Songs of W.E.B. Dubois*, topping out at 800 pages, nests an addiction story within a sweeping historical narrative. Donna Tartt's *The Goldfinch* trades in Dickensian narrative, following its orphaned hero from New York to Amsterdam and tucking in coming-of-age and criminal suspense along the way. All these books have done well, supporting my writers' colony friend who advised women to write tomes. But for me, none of them resonates. They lack the two qualities that keep me returning to *The Man Who Loved Children*: a mesmerizing, explosive use of language, and a refusal, despite all temptation, to indulge in sentimentality.

I can't recall how old I was when I began to suspect sentimentality was not a positive trait. My father was sentimental, and his cruelty seemed inextricable from his sentimentality. I recall a moment in the car, driving home from some school event, when he asked my mother when I would start wearing gloves to such things. My mother—never a sentimentalist—laughed at such an old-fashioned notion, and my father exploded. The manufactured emotion that we associate with sentimentality was, in him, a fragile, brittle shield over the insecurities he divulges all through his diary, and his defense of that shield snapped like a whip.

Sam's baby-names for all his children, but especially Louie, are likewise sentimental and can inch close to cruelty. "Looloo-dirl," he calls her, "Loogoobrious," "Loochus." My father liked to call me "Loos-poos-woos-goose," which put me in mind of honking geese and their droppings. For a very short time, in my twenties, I was married to a sentimental man who called me Lulu and referred to me—fondly, I think—as a little goat. For weeks every December, he played recordings of Christmas carols; one year he gave me a handpainted German nutcracker for a present. All these men could swing suddenly, without warning, into lacerating insults and physical violence. This shouldn't be surprising; history is full of similar examples. Mussolini considered Hitler a sentimentalist. Tony Soprano, the murderous gang leader in *The Sopranos*, weeps over his mother and bemoans the loss of traditions.

At the same time, as a budding writer like Louie, a sponge soaking up literature, theatre, music and poetry, I was a sucker for sentimentality. Bingeing on fantasies of

British history, I yearned for Galahad; I dreamed of the last arrow Robin Hood shot, to let Maid Marian know he'd been betrayed; my heart swelled with the innocence and cruel fate visited upon Lady Jane Grey. Moving into the twentieth century, I wept through Herman Wouk's schmaltzy two-volume docudrama of World War II (another pair of books plucked from my father's shelves). As I was going around the house one Christmas singing "In the Bleak Midwinter," the setting of the Christina Rossetti poem, one of my parents' guests said it was the sappiest carol she knew, and my gut contracted.

When we first meet Louie, she is "hunched over a book . . . so still that she seemed alone in the house." I remember such moments, when everything tangible around me receded and I seemed to enter a book the way C.S. Lewis's Lucy enters Narnia, through the back of a closet. Juxtaposed against Louie's reading is the sentimental Sam, just outside, whispering "Mother Earth, I love you, I love men and women. I love little children and all innocent things, I love, I feel I am love itself." As Dorothy Parker wrote of the too-cute verse of Milne's Winnie-the-Pooh, "Tonstant Weader fwowed up." And yet when we return to Louie, we learn that the book absorbing her is *The Legend of Roncesvalles*, the story of the fabled French hero Roland, who defends the Frankish troops against the treacherous Saracens until at last, sounding his elephant-ivory horn to summon Charlemagne from thirty leagues away, he blows so hard that his arteries burst and he is carried up to heaven. When Sam discovers the book, he warns, "Don't let it give you the idea, Louie, that there's romance in those old savages"—but Sam, who romanticizes "savages" and "the path of human understanding," exemplifies the very sentimentality he disparages. Immediately when he is alone in this scene, he resorts to the cliché "least said, soonest mended" and then blathers on about human nature, human motives, the springs of human action, and the "light pouring forth" from the secretary he wants to have sex with. For sentimentality, Roland doesn't hold a candle to Sam Pollit.

When I first read *The Man Who Loved Children*, I was still in that swamp of sentimentality that most writers need to enter before they can write like themselves. I had been teased enough to know how trite it was to weep over a fallen sparrow or ennoble a medieval crusader, but I hadn't found a way to cope with sentimentality beyond either indulging in it or snarking at it. Stead's greatest gift to a reader like me was perhaps to show me the way out. There are two sentimentalists in this most unsentimental of novels—Sam, who is cruel, and Louie, who is a young writer. Stead seems to set Sam up for our loathing. Yet within all the bracing bluntness of the prose, within the fatal war that Stead grinds inexorably through *The Man Who Loved Children*, she still takes Louisa seriously, because she loves Louisa. If sentimentality is the manufacture of cheap emotion, its opposite—its antidote—is love.

There's an inherent contradiction, of course, in loving your characters. Regardless of the autobiographical nature of your story—and Stead's reflects and refracts her early life in Australia, just as *Philip's Girl* did my young adult life in California—you are manufacturing your characters on the page. If you manufacture a character, if you write so as to get your readers to feel one way or another about that character, are you not also manufacturing emotion? Isn't the novel almost by definition sentimental?

What *The Man Who Loved Children* taught me was the hard, honest, unflattering nature of authentically loving your characters. We all know what this means in real life. The feckless, shoplifting son, the heroin-addicted parent, the narcissistic sister. We may put conditions on giving them money or letting them live with us, but we love them (if we love them) unconditionally. We don't pretend they are better people than they are; if we love them more than our own reputation, we don't whitewash them in front of others to curry favor. Since many (if not most) of our protagonists are based on ourselves, the first task is to love ourselves this way. This quandary may be the reason why novel-writing is a slow-maturing art. As a young person, I swung wildly among the poles of hate, pity, pride, and shame for myself. Consequently I padded my characters with fateful illness, frail beauty, unjust circumstances—whatever I thought would excite sympathy in my reader.

Creative writing teachers and literary agents proved of little help in cutting through the sentimentality. My characters needed to be likable, they insisted. The best way for a character to become likable was for someone else in the book to like him or her. So my characters acquired an admiring younger sister or a best friend at school. If the character was female, she needed to care about others; she needed to nurture. Ambition alone was a negative. Insecurity about one's identity or attractiveness was fine, but not combined with a robust libido, as it is in the protagonists of the big male-authored books I came to know as a young adult—Bellow's Herzog and

Henderson, Updike's Rabbit, Roth's Philip. Most difficult of all was to create a female protagonist who actually had agency—who, that is, could make things happen rather than having things happen to her. Without agency, they were pitiable, and pity is the underside not of love but of hatred. With agency, they posed a threat that had to be ameliorated by the best friend, the children, the others who needed her.

Here's what Stead knows: Liking a character is not the same as loving them. And an author's love for her characters is not the same as a reader's. I have close friends and family members whom I love deeply, knowing their flaws about as well as flaws can be known, and while I sometimes wish that others loved these people as I do, the absence of that love doesn't impinge on mine. Instinctively, as a young writer, I knew these were the people I wanted to conjure in my fiction—not my actual family members, but beings made of words about whom I felt the same way. But how to get there?

In her biography of Christina Stead, Hazel Rowley writes that creating *The Man Who Loved Children* caused Stead extreme distress:

The East 22nd Street apartment was dark

and dreary, overshadowed by high rises with factories on the ground floor. Her internal world—far more oppressive—was overshadowed by her father. The memories came flooding back. She slept badly. She raged. She wept. Among all that masonry, she was effectively undertaking her own psychoanalysis. . . . Writing about her past made her examine her childhood clinically, from the outside. It crystallised the misery of it all: her father's failure to put himself in her place, his fundamental indifference.[30]

Samuel Pollit differs from David Stead in several details—David Stead's erudition, his "verbal pyrotechnics," and of course his nationality, since the entire novel was relocated from Australia to the United States. But Sam Pollit's language and personality were both, according to David Stead's wife, "substantially true."

Does Stead love not only Louisa, but also the monster of the book, Sam Pollit? I have two observations here— one from the biography, the other from my own writing struggles.

Clearly David Stead did plenty to engender

resentment and even hatred in his daughter. He was extremely handsome and chagrined by her plain looks; he considered them a kind of deformity. He mocked and humiliated Christina even as his own efforts to gain respect in scientific circles kept falling short. He was a white supremacist and eugenicist. He never accorded Christina an iota of respect for the work she did, both to earn his approval and to make a name for herself as a writer. During her adolescence he taunted and tortured her. According to Hazel Rowley, "David Stead shared Pollit's inability to recognize other people as separate entities, with minds of their own."[31] Early Australian reviewers of the novel, as well as members of Stead's family, were shocked by the "tremendously cruel" portrait of Sam Pollit even as they recognized its veracity. And yet Stead wrote to her stepmother, Thistle, of *The Man Who Loved Children*, "I'm not unforgiving—how could it be so when no-one is to blame?—they just made an etching out of me. I am deep-bitten."[32] And in one of the rare interviews she granted, late in her life, she spoke fondly of her father.

In fact, what makes the book tragic, for me, is how hard not only Louisa but also her creator work to give Sam Pollit some moments of redemption. In these moments we recognize that the project of the book isn't to make us hate Sam but to describe the arc of Louisa's particular creative life, an arc that necessarily includes the trauma that being Sam's daughter induces in her. Sentimentality isn't just roses and soft waftings of music; it includes the deliberate stirring up of revulsion or hatred as well. As the Dickensian scholar Juliet John puts it, "The villains of nineteenth-century melodrama are types struggling to become individuals."[33] Struggling and failing, I might add, and it's that predetermined failure that makes them easy to sentimentalize.

In Stead's novel, by contrast, Sam's individuality keeps breaking through, complicating everything. Yes, he's a sadist who loves setting his children upon one another; yes, he beats his wife; yes, he demeans and suffocates Louie. But when his sister Jo storms in to condemn their younger sister Bonnie for seeing a married man, Sam says calmly: "Jo, you are not the avenging angel, you must be human in these matters. . . . I understand how you feel. But you are wrong, believe me; you cannot dragoon human beings. . . . It is kindness, human love, and patience with human weakness that is necessary. Remember this is your own sister, ten years my junior, and I know little enough how to run my own affairs!"

Other times, when Sam has gone on about love and kindness, we've seen what a thin veil the words are over his authoritarianism. But here, he's right, and his humility feels genuine. Later, Stead writes from his point of view just before a fight with Henny: "Sam was taking hold of himself, and a surge of compassion, not only for himself, nor for Henny, but for the misery of all such souls wedded to bondage, rushed up." The compassion won't linger long, but it feels genuine, a moment of contradictory impulses in Sam rather than just an instance of the bad faith we see when he's lecturing Louie about his high ideals or eternal victimization. To some degree, Stead's ability to mark this compassion and not have it tumble into sentimentality is a consequence of what critics call her excess. That is, by immersing us readers in the horrifying scenes of Sam's narcissism and cruelty, she can individualize him without expiating his sins or giving him a hero's journey.

More than once, Stead refers to Sam as a child. The word doesn't exactly comport with the man who rapes his wife or glories in the thought of selective genocide, but it echoes the book's title. If Sam Pollit is the man who loves children, then all he can embrace in himself is the eternal child, with all the cruelty and petulance that childishness permits.

Finally, even after Sam has proved himself every bit the villain of the book, Stead gives him a moment of real, un-ironized virtue. When Jo announces that she's given Bonnie's baby away and thrown Bonnie out, for once Sam and Henny take the same side. After Henny declares that she'll "go and walk the streets with that poor miserable brat sister of yours," Sam joins in:

> "Shut up, Jo: the trouble with you is you don't understand anything and you don't try to learn.... I will get Bonnie out of your place. I'll bring her down here. Jo, you must try to be kinder. You are beyond human life."

Sam's tragedy isn't that he is a fundamentally evil man, nor that he is that classic figure with a "fatal flaw." Instead we shake our heads at him, especially in these rare, softer moments, and say the way we would say to a cruelly dysfunctional member of the family, "My god, you're impossible." Impossible but alive, a paradox of a human being, a sentimentalist unsentimentally recreated. His tragedy lies with those who can't get quit of him— including Louisa, who can't bring herself to poison him in the end. Nor could Stead, because she, too, loved her impossible father.

All writers draw on their lives—for plots, characters, places, the moral compass of their fiction. Stead used hers directly in *The Man Who Loved Children*, obliquely in her eleven other novels. I have relied on my own life primarily in short stories and memoir, with *Philip's Girl* remaining the only novel that refracts my autobiography in obvious ways. Still, I've always worked toward the bracing realness, the lack of writerly apology I find in *The Man Who Loved Children*. One moment stands out for me, when the way Stead went about creating Sam Pollit gave me the key to unlocking a "villainous" character.

The book I was writing, *Honor* (later retitled *A Sister to Honor* by the publisher, in one of those waves of titles for books by women that seemed to insist on protagonists being labeled as girls, daughters, sisters, mothers), sprang from an intersection of interests in my own life. My younger son was at the time a standout athlete, supported by enthusiastic coaches who gave inspiring speeches about sportsmanship and the honor of clean competition, but who wanted above all else to win.

At the same time, the college where I taught boasted the best men's squash team in America—a strange claim to fame, since squash is little played here outside elite gyms and prep schools. Most of the athletes on the squash team came from British Commonwealth countries, and it was easy to see, away from the squash court, how foreign American culture was for these young men. Just to push the question, I Googled "where do the best squash players come from" and got the answer: northwestern Pakistan, home of the Pashtuns and the Taliban. As I considered the extent to which any of this was material for fiction, I remembered Virginia Woolf's essay about Judith Shakespeare, William Shakespeare's sister. "Let me imagine," Woolf wrote, "since facts are so hard to come by, what would have happened had Shakespeare had a wonderfully gifted sister, called Judith."[34] What, then, I thought, if a talented young squash player, Shahid, from that part of the world, an area riven with honor culture, came to a small college in the United States and brought with him his very bright sister, Afia, who wants to become a doctor? What if she fell in love? What if she fell in love with a Jew?

To research the book I read a dozen books on Pashtun culture, on women in Islam, on honor violence. I read another dozen works of fiction by authors from Pakistan. Finally, I journeyed to the city of Peshawar, in the heart of Pashtun country, where you could hear gunshots at night from the jihadi training camps in the mountains. I lived with a family and came to know them well. I spoke with tribal elders about their daughters and with young women about gender expectations. I developed a plot that I hoped reflected fairly the predicament that such families found themselves in and the chain of events that would lead to tragedy. I had tapped into the complicated and often irrational ideas of honor that pervade the sports culture in which I and my son were steeped. I came to know the Pashtun people, whose points of view I aimed to inhabit, well enough that I saw them not as the demonic figures conjured by the American press but as human, all too human.

One hurdle remained.

I had determined that Afia's stepbrother Khalid—not Shahid, the squash player, but an older guy, whose mother had died and been replaced by another, who had for years harbored repressed desire for his stepsister and envy of his stepbrother, who had found the respect he felt his family owed him in the training camps of jihad—would be the one to uncover evidence of her hidden romance and try to eliminate Afia. But every way I painted Khalid, every excuse I gave him, still resulted in a stock villain, a figure that could be held up as a typically misogynist, reactionary, violent Muslim by readers inclined to think in stereotypes. Then I remembered Stead and her unsentimental novel, her book housing a monster. I remembered how clearly I saw that the author loved Sam Pollit without excuses or softening of his violent, destructive character. She loved him because she knew him, because he was her father.

I sat at the computer and opened a new document. I shut my eyes to hear the voice of a young man I love and will always love. I heard his aggressive insecurity. I heard him quickly paper over an irrational outburst with a loose, transparent weave of others' insults, others' inexcusable behavior, others' unprovoked cruelty to him. I heard his raw jealousy and desperate need to be loved. I felt the bottomless pit that is the hunger of his unsated ego and rickety pride. I saw again the cage that he's built around himself and only locks tighter each time he tries to break free of it. Almost without thinking, I entered Khalid's point of view in the moments after he has accidentally shot his stepbrother instead of his stepsister:

If only Shahid had not stepped forward like that.

If only he had let Khalid get off a shot, a clean shot. The bastard, the stupid arrogant bastard. Get in the middle, get yourself killed.

If only Shahid had played his part, the part Khalid had prepared so lovingly for him. So that he, Shahid, would be the one to cleanse their honor. Yes? Giving Shahid the glory, always giving him the glory.

If only! If only his *badal*, his retribution, had been allowed to proceed slowly, as he had meant it to. If only Uncle Omar had not become involved. There was the bastard: Omar. Pushing, always pushing. It was his fault, that bastard Omar's fault.

I kept going. It broke my heart, now, to see inside Khalid, to understand him so well and to know that I was powerless to keep him from his destructive path. I don't mean to say that I felt I had transformed this fictional character into a young American man; that would be at the least an act of cultural transgression, projecting an American identity onto someone whose culture and sense of identity came from other sources. Rather, what I had learned in Pakistan was that this sort of violence—what we call honor killing—was often perpetrated by male figures who had other issues and other agendas, much as what we call crimes of passion in this country are committed by people who have other impulses or motives. The challenge had been to capture not just the honor culture in which Khalid had been raised but also the gnarled personality that was his alone. It may be arrogant to assume we truly know our characters—who do we truly know in real life?—but hearing a voice we profoundly recognize may be the cleanest way in.

The free indirect discourse I'd started went on, unimpeded, until it ended in a series of rhetorical questions (the young man I love often asks a number of rapid-fire, rhetorical questions, like a talented if wrongheaded debate champion)—*How could . . . ? How could . . . ? How could . . . ?*—and then Khalid's final, transparently empty defense:

What, oh what had he been made to do, when all he desired was purity and his rightful place?

If *A Sister to Honor* succeeds, it does so because of Khalid. He comes by his bad faith honestly, as Sam Pollit does. Like Sam, not all of his impulses are contemptible.

These facts don't excuse or soften him, any more than my love for his real-world counterpart or Christina Stead's love for her father compels either of us to persuade readers to "like" characters who do such grievous harm. But the novel springs free of the trap of sentimentality and—I hope—rouses instead a complex of emotions that readers will feel for themselves. If I've succeeded in this project, it's because of Christina Stead and the hours she spent weeping in that dark New York apartment.

POSTSCRIPT:
WHEN THE BOOK
DOESN'T SELL

THOR AND WHAT CAME AFTER

Publishing fiction is hard. Readership is continually contracting. One's previous sales figures enter the conversation before anyone has a chance to talk about the work at hand. Most editors I know at major publishing houses say they scarcely have time to read manuscripts, so bound up is their day with marketing meetings, publicity meetings, sales meetings, media strategies, potential movie deals. Meetings on Zoom, which began with the coronavirus pandemic and never completely tapered off, take far more time than a quick exchange by the water cooler.

Throughout mainstream publishing, pressure has mounted to present an author who's photogenic, savvy about social media, and in the style of whichever author succeeded last year. The midlist has disappeared, in part due to the consolidation of big-name publishers and in part from the never-ending fallout of *Thor Power Tool Co. v. Commissioner*, a 1979 Supreme Court ruling that eliminated the option to "write down inventory" and thus forced publishers to cut print runs and dispose of slow-selling books before the end of each fiscal year.[35] Hundreds of books that might have slowly increased sales through word of mouth or course adoptions have been pulped instead, leaving only the bestsellers and whatever shiny new object has come along recently. Meanwhile, smaller advances for risk-taking books mean that publishing houses have little investment in the "product" and will do nothing to seek out readers. Then there's Amazon, whose dealmaking ensures that only formula-adherent blockbuster novels will reach their 200 million Prime subscribers.

Earlier I mentioned that I'm doubtful of Jarrell's conclusion that the mediocre rollout of *The Man Who Loved Children* deprived Stead's readers of the great books she would have gone on to write had that novel achieved renown. To that doubt I'll add another claim. I have published eleven books, most of them fiction, one or two mildly successful and the others well below the radar. I have five full-length novel manuscripts in my file cabinet that may never see the light of day, one of them the casualty of a publishing relationship so toxic that I bought the rights back rather than letting them bring the book out as a travesty of what I had spent a decade creating. When you have been at this as long as I have, there's little ambition left just to get the book between hard covers and into the hands of friends. If I—or the writers I know and respect—could make our language shatter glass as Stead's does and could hew so close to the bone of truth that sentimentality would have no way to sneak in, we would find ourselves satisfied, regardless of whether the publishing world chews us up or spits us out.

I would, anyway.

What actually happens when a novel underperforms? What actually happens when it performs beyond anyone's wildest dreams? Herman Melville and Thomas Hardy both wrote poetry almost exclusively in their later years—but Hardy's novels had sold like hotcakes (giving him financial freedom to write poetry) while Melville lugged home hundreds of unsold copies of *Moby-Dick* and turned to poetry as a failed novelist.

Let's set aside, for starters, those writers who find a commercially successful formula and stick to it. I'm not trying to be a snob here, but I don't believe a question about how success emboldens or stifles a writer's imagination applies when what you're seeking is not a wider range or a deeper palette but rather a system that works. Let's look, instead, at a writer like Junot Diaz, whose debut book of short stories, *Drown*, became a runaway bestseller and a staple in college courses. Expectations ran high that a great novel would quickly follow. Instead, according to Diaz, he pulled back, certain that he wasn't ready to meet those expectations. He spent years writing a science-fiction novel before finally abandoning it and turning instead to a sci-fi-loving character in his Pulitzer Prize-winning novel *The Brief Wondrous Life of Oscar Wao*.

Kate Atkinson also hit pay dirt with her first novel, *Behind the Scenes at the Museum*, but she didn't wait. She came out with *Human Croquet* two years later, followed by *Emotionally Weird*. Then she swerved into a detective series for more than a decade before she came up with the stunning *Life after Life*, which makes all the earlier work seem like practice. If success freed her to write that amazing book, it's not obvious that it did so right away, or that the novel didn't emerge simply from all the work she had been doing, year after year.

Kiran Desai, by contrast, won the Booker Prize with her sophomore novel, *The Inheritance of Loss*, in 2006 and has published nothing since.

On the flip side, stories of authors who faced rejection or whose early books sold poorly before they "broke out" form the lore that keeps MFA graduates pecking away at their laptops. J.R.R. Tolkien had trouble finding a publisher for *Lord of the Rings*. Stephen King's *Carrie* was rejected thirty times. John Irving was a midlist author with three tepidly received novels under his belt when he came out with *The World According to Garp*. Arguments abound as to whether he has grown into our era's Dickens since then or whether he has fallen into mannered repetition, with a few too many bear cameos in his eleven subsequent novels. F. Scott Fitzgerald was seen as an author who might write something great one day but hadn't yet—a judgment that continued through the slow sales of *The Great Gatsby* but didn't stop Fitzgerald from daring to write it.

As a midlist writer myself, I question my own assessments of those writers who seem able to put their grocery lists between hard covers and get a fat advance. With that caveat, I'll venture that the work of writers I follow closely has tended to lapse after big success, at least for a while. Sometimes the subsequent work feels like a less inventive reiteration of the novel that brought acclaim.

Sometimes the rollout has felt rushed, as if the pressure to keep one's name in the public eye has overwhelmed the writer's instinct to revise, restructure, ratchet up the stakes. Sometimes it seems fatigue has set in—and why not? Writing the best novel you're capable of takes an infuriating amount of time, wasted drafts, darlings killed, backache and neckache, nausea at your own prose. If the critics and the reading public are telling you that what you've got is gold already, why keep mining?

I also know writers who have either given up or have turned to chamber pieces, chapbooks and self-published work and small-press musings, and while I would not label these writers failures, I wonder if a healthier balance of encouragement and expectations wouldn't have awakened a greater genius in them.

WRITING THE BOOK YOU WANT TO WRITE

From the perspective of 2023, Christina Stead's career seems remarkable. At the age of twenty-seven, she sent the manuscript of her first, poetic novel, *Seven Poor Men of Sydney*, to various publishers in France, England, and the United States. No agent, no auction; one original typescript sent at a time. Peter Davies, just starting his publishing house in London, finally picked it up, but he was more interested in Stead's potential than the book itself, and he insisted she write something else to be published ahead of *Seven Poor Men*. She satisfied this demand by quickly writing *The Salzburg Tales*, a Boccaccio-inspired series of stories, after she had given up on writing a more conventional novel. Hazel Rowley, Stead's biographer, writes, "In terms of technical and imaginative brilliance she would never surpass this early book," but by the time it came out, Stead herself was "quite dissatisfied with the kindergarten style of *The Salzburg Tales*."[36] Hers was a minority opinion; the book received wide review coverage, all of it positive. *Seven Poor Men*, on the other hand, required another year of revision and still landed with a dull thud. Reviewers of course saw it as a follow-up, not a predecessor, to *The Salzburg Tales* and compared it unfavorably—exactly the kind of second-book comparison that prompted Junot Diaz to wait more than a decade after publishing *Drown*.

Stead herself reacted like a born writer, disappointed and resigned to continuing a life of writing books:

Nobody likes it very much: no doubt they will like the following ones in a harmonious crescendo of dubiety and slam: can't be helped. As long as Davies or some other keeps publishing I can hope to strike it lucky one day.[37]

Here is where Stead's career starts to confound a simplistic notion of success or failure and their effect on a writer's future output. She kept writing. She tussled with a novel eventually called *The Beauties and Furies*, which was in part about a failed love affair she'd had and in part about how beauty itself enthralls. She received endless revision suggestions from Peter Davies, who also gave her no advance for the book. She felt the way I have felt too many times about novels I've revised in an effort to please my agent or satisfy my publisher—that the genius of the story had become lost, and that what Stead called Davies's "library of objections" had resulted in books that were no longer singular but "rehashes." "I thirst to do something so good," she wrote a friend, "that there will be no denying it on anyone's part."[38] That's an impossible goal; it's also every writer's goal.

But Stead's literary world, in 1934, was different from mine in 2023. She had dinner with an editor in New York, who introduced her to Max Schuster, one of the founders of Simon & Schuster, and next thing she knew, a bidding war had started for the American rights to her novel as well as for the next three-book contract.

Agents weren't involved. Marketing departments weren't involved. Book reviews appeared in all major newspapers, and readers followed them for recommendations. Reviews for *The Beauties and Furies* were mixed, but no death knell sounded for Stead's career, because prior to the *Thor* ruling, the books didn't have to sell or be pulped by the end of the fiscal year. She felt free to embark on a big book, *House of All Nations*, whose gritty tapestry wove the realistic schemes of crooked capitalists with pervasive references to myth and dark magic.

Here, though, she ran into frustrations familiar to me and to plenty of contemporary writers, regardless of how multilayered and market-driven our publishing world has become. Clifton Fadiman, her editor, praised the writing but warned her that she "overwhelmed the reader." He wanted her to cut, condense, reshape. Suddenly her book felt rudderless, her protagonists floundering. The book came out with good publicity and a fine cover, but Simon & Schuster printed only 3,000 copies to start with and then reprinted only 9,000; Peter Davies apparently dampened their enthusiasm with his disappointment in the final book, which sold poorly in England. In a note whose tone is familiar to me, he wrote to Stead, "I do not think it a book, or perhaps even the sort of book, which you ought to write if you desire either fame or success."[39]

This kind of response is hardly encouraging. And yet the next thing that Stead wrote didn't follow Davies's or Fadiman's prescriptions. It was *The Man Who Loved Children*.

The intrusions of editors on Stead's imaginative canvas ring a bell for me. As I'm rehearsing the arc of her career here, the conundrum hits me hard. Of how many books do we say, "Wow, that could have used an editor!" (I'm looking at you, Hanya Yanagihara.) As Brian Evenson pointed out in *Raymond Carver's What We Talk About When We Talk About Love*, his account of Carver's work for this same Bookmarked series, the editor Gordon Lish gets credit for much of what we consider brilliant in Carver's writing—and yet Carver preferred versions of his stories that Lish hadn't tampered with, and Evenson himself resents what Lish does to his own work.

I mentioned above that my first five novels were brought out more or less unedited. I wasn't vain as a writer. I wanted editorial input. Rereading the books years later, I'm sure they'd have benefited from it. Yet after the manuscript of what would have been my sixth novel went through several massive rounds of editing (change third person to first person; change first person to multiple first-person points of view; widen the timeline from two years to twenty years; change the multiple perspectives from three to four and change from first person to third person; eliminate the final third of the book; return to a unitary third person from a different point of view; write a new ending; write a new beginning; and so on), I had lost the thread of what was to have woven the book in the first place. When the publisher slapped an absurd cover on the final product, it gave me only relief to buy back the manuscript.

Working with agents and editors on subsequent books—and I write now *in medias res*—has released wellsprings of imagination but has just as often led me down dead ends and produced scenes and characters in the final, published versions that bring me a hollow sense of embarrassment. To illustrate what I mean, it's perhaps best to focus on a book that has not seen the light of day. Some years ago, at the college where I taught, an official narrative of a shocking event clashed with what everyone seemed to know was the truth. In the official narrative, a fraternity president was found beaten almost to death by Latino thugs in the poor neighborhood adjacent to the school. When the college's president called for scrutiny of the fraternities, alumni rose up with calls for his firing and for secure gates to be built around the campus to keep out these violent undesirables. In the underground narrative, however, the frat president had raped the girlfriend of a member of a rival frat. She and several of her friends had gathered up their high heels and persuaded a couple of guys to find where the aggressor and a friend were walking back to campus from a party. The guys chased off the friend; the women beat the rapist with their heels and left him unconscious, bleeding heavily, with a concussion and a broken jaw. Local residents, Latino or otherwise, had nothing to do with the crime beyond reporting it to the police. The women were never charged, though everyone knew who they were.

The story seemed ripe for a murder mystery, where assumptions about class, race, gender expectations, #MeToo, and the status quo all play their part in a world I know only too well. I took most of a year to write a first draft that excited me. I'd never written a mystery, and this one played with reader expectations in ways that upped the ante.

Then the editorial process began. Little by little, cut

by cut, tangent by tangent, in exchanges between my agent and me, the story began to twist into something I wasn't sure I recognized. I had been through this process enough times by now. Finally I wrote to ask my agent (who wanted still more revisions before he would send the book out) what he thought the book was about. He replied that it was about a great showdown between the college and its biggest benefactor, who was the frat president's father, and that this benefactor would withhold funds and drive the college into bankruptcy if they didn't find and convict his son's killers. When I pointed out that none of that appeared in my novel, nor did the issues or characters he brought up intrigue me as either a reader or a writer, he echoed Peter Davies's advice to Christina Stead. His main claim to fame, he argued, had been helping several novelists to grow rich. He had advised these now-wealthy writers not to do the things I was aiming for in my book, but rather to follow his guidance and please the readers he knew best. He aspired to the same success for me.

I tucked that manuscript away. I changed agents. Though I had read and taught *The Man Who Loved Children* many times, I didn't know about Stead's struggles with her editors. If I had, I might have recognized the signs even sooner. I might have seen how easily literary loneliness and the thirst for support can snuff out a vision. I might have understood how stubborn and peculiar a writer must be to engage fully in the editorial wrestling match and still pin the story.

THE MAN WHO LOVED CHILDREN

The big change Stead made to please the editors of *The Man Who Loved Children* was to shift the story from Australia to the United States. As with revisions to her other novels, she embarked on the change reluctantly, but managed to make it without losing the fiery vision of the book. That Clifton Fadiman, once her editor, reviewed the book in *The New Yorker* seems unethical to us now, but what's interesting to me is that he voices the same kinds of criticism that he had made while editing Stead:

> Her prose is difficult, often unnecessarily so. Her characters are like so many fiends. Her books are long, perhaps too long. They do not develop out of one another but are massively solitary. Her humor is savage, her learning hard to cope with, her fancies too furious.[40]

Too many notes, again. Fadiman extols Stead's earlier

work, *The Salzburg Tales* and *The House of All Nations*, in which he'd had a hand. He still writes, "No one interested in our literature can afford to neglect her," but his admiration feels strained by disappointment. I suspect Stead was more pleased, despite its reservations, with the *New York Times* review by Charles Poore, which begins,

> It would be imprudent to suppose from the title's serenity that Mis Stead has written a hymn to the hearth and the home. On the contrary. Miss Stead carries her allergy to sentiment to powerful extremes. . . . The words move in a *danse macabre*, but they dance.[41]

Randall Jarrell's question, twenty-five years later, is whether the lukewarm reception of *The Man Who Loved Children* flattened the rest of Stead's output, depriving the rest of us of the astounding literature she might have created otherwise. Certainly it deprived readers of *The Man Who Loved Children*. "The moment was unpropitious," Hazel Rowley writes with understatement of the book's release on the eve of World War II; by the end of the war it would be out of print, not to be seen again until Randall Jarrell discovered it in 1965.

Here, too, I feel an affinity with Stead. Exactly twenty-five years passed between the initial publication of my post-Roe dystopia, *The Misconceiver*, and its rediscovery in 2022, in a post-Dobbs world. I know well the satisfaction in having the world give your work a second, more beneficent look. I also know what regret you can feel for the unfulfilled hopes you had for the book when it was first born, when you were the writer you were then and you tried to launch your great boat of a novel onto waiting seas of readers. That moment can never return.

I find no evidence, though, that disappointing sales and reviews of *The Man Who Loved Children* affected Stead's ambition or range. At first, apparently, she hoped to write something less personally painful. But she had seized on anger as an engine of imagination, and as she wrote her next book, *Letty Fox: Her Luck*, a story about a young woman's desires and the sexual economics that drive marriage, she wrote to her husband, "I feel splendid, nastier, and more Stead-ish each day." Her novel *For Love Alone*, which actually appeared before *Letty Fox*, was transparently a sequel to *The Man Who Loved Children*, but with few compromises; for one thing, it begins in Australia. She shifted publishers, first to Little, Brown and then to Viking. Yes, she remained a midlist author, contending at every turn with the degrees to which her work departed from commercial expectations. Simon & Schuster had urged her to write something more similar to *Gone with the Wind* (the same advice, incidentally, I received in 2010); Viking wanted her to write more like John Steinbeck. "This is the sort of nonsense I have to stand each time a book is a best-seller," she wrote to a friend. "May the word perish." Her new literary agent, like my former one, was always "telling me how right the publishers are and advising me how to write." She received no big advances. Like F. Scott Fitzgerald and countless others, she went to Hollywood to write screenplays for money.

On the other side were the small tribe of Christina Stead fans, and they, too, were disappointed, but not— or not at first—by her writing. Jose Yglesias followed her career closely and wrote in *The Nation*:

> When *For Love Alone* came out in 1946— inevitably bound, it seemed, for the 49-cent remainder counter at the Concord bookstores— some of us who had been reading Christina Stead for years argued about why it received no attention. We finally decided the jacket

cover—for we were optimists then—was the reason serious readers were not being drawn to it. The critics, we knew, only followed fashions. When *Letty Fox, Her Luck* came out two years later with a romantic cameo drawing of a pretty girl on the cover . . . we shook our heads at Christina Stead's shortsightedness in allowing her publishers to misrepresent her work. In the next six years, she published two more novels, neither as ambitious as her previous one. . . . By then, like disappointed lovers, we were using the faults in Christina Stead's work to explain why her novels had never caught on.[42]

In other words, if you assign a book the status of genius and then find subsequent books not marketed well or selling well, you will slowly turn away from blaming the publisher and start blaming—and reevaluating—the author.

For real writers—by which I mean those of us condemned to write regardless of the fates of our efforts—two things can be simultaneously true. One is that we are buoyed by positive reception. After 1952, Stead could not find a publisher to take on her work. Then, following

Randall Jarrell's 1965 rediscovery of *The Man Who Loved Children*, she sold two novels she had been revising for years to publishers in the States and the U.K., and she confessed to a fresh burst of energy. At the same time, the notion that a rave review or a return to print will find us writers "walking on air," as Harold Bloom wrote to Stead in 1965, feels wrongheaded. Stead wrote to Jarrell after reading his introduction,

> Thank you for recreating that book for me and making me able to read it with some creative feeling. The worst thing about books for the author is that once done, he can't bear to look at them again, not only for their errors, the incredible oversights and indiscipline, but also that they are no longer creative, they are dead.[43]

What lies ahead, in other words, isn't the book getting the praise, but the next one, the one that demands your soul again and returns no guarantees. I felt exactly like Stead when *The Misconceiver* was rediscovered and picked up by a publisher. Hearing the news, friends told me they were sure I now had a bestseller on my hands, that this would be my great breakthrough. But what I felt was ninety percent gratitude and ten percent faith. Gratitude for having the book "recreated," as Stead put it, and allowing both me and others to read it in a fresh light. Faith that the years spent making a book whose public life would be cut short by the financial considerations provoked by the *Thor* ruling might not be entirely wasted.

What does not lie ahead is any promise that the next book you write will be greater or more daring than the last. If that were so, then the years of missed reviews, struggles with publishers, and weak sales would have blocked Stead from writing *The Man Who Loved Children* in the first place. And yet she wrote it. She next wrote *Letty Fox: Her Luck*, her best-selling novel, daring in its portrait of sexuality (and sometimes banned for it), which some critics today rank above *The Man Who Loved Children*. She wrote through fourteen years of publishing drought. After the acclaim accorded to *The Man Who Loved Children* in 1965, she published three more novels during her lifetime. One of them, *Cotters' England*, seemed to the English novelist Angela Carter at least as good as *The Man Who Loved Children*, and others compared it to work by Dostoevsky, but it was panned in the *New York Times* and sold poorly.

Stead died as a celebrated but little-known writer.

Some of her books, both before and after she received public acclaim and critical studies, worked better than others. As with most writers whose reputations linger after their deaths, she is known today for one book, *The Man Who Loved Children*. But for her, the book was part of a writer's life, a thing she wrung herself dry to produce and then gave to the world to judge.

THE LAST WORD

Again and again, in essays that praise or take exception to *The Man Who Loved Children*, its author is described as strange. Critics assume this strangeness and go to some lengths to explain it. Was Stead a closet lesbian? Why did she continue to be so angry throughout her life? Why did she persist in being what her editor deemed "commercially difficult"?

She doesn't seem strange to me. The world she created in *The Man Who Loved Children* is extreme. Both its heroine and its monster go to extremes. Most of all, its language is extreme. But for me, language is divine, and everything divine calls for extremes. I was brought up in the Episcopal church and earned a Girl Scout badge for finishing the King James Bible, and the one sentence that sang and continues to sing to me from all those years is the first line of the Book of John: *In the beginning was the Word, and the Word was with God, and the Word was God.* That was the ticket, I thought. Language was the essence of divinity. To make a thing of words, you have to work that essence; you have to risk the fate of Prometheus, who stole fire from the gods. You have to place yourself in an encounter with the sublime as Burke defined it three hundred years ago, something as terrifying as it is desired. The characters Stead built from words have given me more each time I've read the book. In the first instance, Sam Pollit gave me permission to abhor my own thin-skinned, dictatorial father; later, he helped me understand where my father and so many other fathers had come from, buffeted by the presumptions and disappointments of the first half of the twentieth century, especially the Depression; still later, he convinced me that love of a character could free a writer from sentimentalizing them. Louisa, meanwhile, gave me back myself, even in those secret places where I had always felt shame or embarrassment. Henny challenged me to love her, and I did, and it gives me delight to whisper to critics who still call her spoiled, nagging, shrewish, *No, no, no and no, you imbeciles, no.*

But more than characters or plot, *The Man Who Loved*

Children gave me the possibilities of what a writer could do with language if she dared. She could sketch the drowning of a cat by a lonely twelve-year-old as lightly as a rune ("Louie felt a sort of sickness. . . . The cat took a long time to drown"). She could put horrific bigotry into the mouth of a grown man using baby talk. She could render gossip about death as fanciful as chatter about fashion. She could endow despair and fury with an entire poetic lexicon and then turn on a dime to describe violence with clinical detachment ("Sam hit her, with his open hand, across the mouth"). She could translate the intelligence and acumen of children onto the page without sacrificing their childishness or fragility. And when she has earned her black belt, as it were, in language, she can free herself into beauty, as with the passage at the book's end:

> She smiled, felt light as a dolphin undulating through the waves, one of those beautiful, large, sleek marine mammals that plunged and wallowed, with their clever eyes. As she crossed the bridge (looking back and seeing none of the Naval Academy as yet on their little beach, or scrambling down the sodden bluff), she heaved

a great breath. How different everything looked, like the morning of the world.

This is what I want, more than any of the fame or fortune others have dangled before me as they did before Christina Stead: to make of words that sublime world, crowded with all its strange people, that only I can make.

ENDNOTES

1. Hazel Rowley, *Christina Stead: A Biography* (NY: Henry Holt, 1993), p. 258.

2. Clifton Fadiman, "Christina Stead Continues," *The New Yorker*, 19 Oct. 1940, p. 104.

3. Louis B. Salomon, "Scalpel, Please," The Nation, 26 Oct. 1940, p. 399; Charles Poore, *New York Times*, 18 Oct. 1940, p. 19; Mary McCarthy, "Framing Father," *New Republic*, 104:2, 13 Jan. 1941, p. 16.

4. Randall Jarrell, "An Unread Book," in *Christina Stead, The Man Who Loved Children* (NY: Henry Holt, 1965), p. xxxix.

5. Letter to Thistle Harris, 7 July 1939, in *Stead, A Web of Friendship: Selected Letters (1928 – 1973)* (Carlton, Australia: Miegunyah Press, 1992), p. 101.

6. Jarrell, v; xvi.

7. Jonathan Franzen, "A Strindberg Family Robinson," *New York Times Book Review*, 6 June 2010, p. 11.

8. Franzen, 11.

9. Jarrell, xxxii.

10. Jose Yglesias, "Marx as Muse," *The Nation*, 5 April 1965, p. 369.

11. Michael Ackland, "Socialists of a New Socialism?" *ELH*, 78:2, Summer 2011, p. 389.

12. Angela Carter, "Unhappy Families," *London Review of Books* 4:17, 16 September 1982.

13 Jane Smiley, "Thirteen Ways of Looking at the Novel (NY: Knopf, 2005), p. 488.

14. David Lodge, *The Art of Fiction* (NY: Viking, 1992), p. 26.

15. Stead, *Selected Letters*, 535.

16. De Kretser's remarks on the novel, in an illuminating lecture and discussion, are part of a series on Australian literature hosted by Ramona Koval: https://www.youtube.com/watch?v=jTd0cXuDI7c.

17. De Kretser ibid.

18. A number of studies focus on the evolving shape of American masculinity in the first half of the twentieth century, especially during the Depression. Encyclopedia.com contains a thought-provoking study of the Depression's impact on gender roles and sexual relations, which points out the preference for so-called Negro work

over women's work (https://www.encyclopedia.com/ economics/encyclopedias-almanacs-transcripts-and-maps/ gender-roles-and-sexual-relations-impact-great-depression). Other works examining the pressures on men and their responses to those pressures in this period include Conor Heffernan's "Building husky bodies: Strenuous masculinity in post-Depression America" (*European Journal of American Culture* 40: June 2021, 105–120); Josep M. Armengol's "Gendering the Great Depression: rethinking the male body in 1930s American culture and literature" (*Journal of Gender Studies*, 23:1, 2014, 59–68); and Brandon Locke's "American Manhood" in *The Military-Masculinity Complex: Hegemonic Masculinity and the American Armed Forces*, at brandontlocke.com.

19. Oliver Wendell Holmes, Opinion of the Court, p. 3, at https://www.docsteach.org/documents/document/supreme-court-opinion-buck-v-bell.

20. Rosellen Brown, "Don't Just Sit There," *New England Review* 13:1 (1990), p. 88.

21. Leonhardt's succinct assessment of *The Golden Bough* as anthropology appears in his review of John Vickery, *The Literary Impact of The Golden Bough* (*The Review of English Studies*, 26:1, February 1975, p. 97).

22. Madeleine Schwartz, "I don't even get bananas," *London Review of Books*, 39:21, 2 November 2017.

23. Letter to Richard Kopley, in Stead, *Selected Letters*, 525.

24. Letter to Florence James, cited in Rowley, *Christina Stead*, 159.

25. Alice Walker, "One Child of One's Own," in Janet Sternberg, ed., *The Writer on Her Work* (NY: Norton, 2000), p. 121.

26. Lauren Sandler, "The Secret to Being Both a Successful Writer and a Mother: Have Just One Kid," *The Atlantic*, 7 June 2013. Commenting on the piece in the magazine and on Twitter, authors Zadie Smith, Jane Smiley, Aimee Phan, and Ayelet Waldman, among others, objected, pointing out in Phan's words that "The support network the woman has in order to have both family and writing is what is most important."

27. The website LitHub devoted an article to both male and female writers' views on having children, and King weighed in on the pro side.
https://lithub.com/14-famous-writers-on-whether-or-not-to-have-kids.

28. Jarrell, Introduction to Stead, *The Man Who Loved Children*, xxxvi.

29. Gustave Flaubert, *Madame Bovary*, trans. Paul de Man (New York: Norton, 1965), p. 49.

30. Rowley, *Christina Stead*, 258.

31. Rowley, *Christina Stead*, 50.

32. Stead, *Selected Letters*, 101.

33. Juliet John, *Dickens's Villains: Melodrama, Character, and Popular Culture* (Oxford: Oxford University Press, 2001), p. 49.

34. Virginia Woolf, *A Room of One's Own* (New York: Harcourt, 1929), p. 80.

35. A useful summary of the Thor decision itself as well as its impact on book publishing is in Kevin O'Donnell's "How Thor Power Hammered Publishing," at https://www.sfwa.org/2005/01/05/how-thor-power-hammered-publishing/.

36. Rowley, *Christina Stead*, 152.

37. Letter to Florence James, cited in Rowley, *Christina Stead*, 161.

38. Letter to Nettie Palmer, cited in Rowley, *Christina Stead*, 201.

39. Rowley, *Christina Stead*, 247.

40. Clifton Fadiman, "Christina Stead Continues," 104–5.

41. Poore, 19.

42. Jose Yglesias, "Marx as Muse," 368-9

43. Letter to Randall Jarrell, cited in Rowley, *Christina Stead*, 447.

OTHER
BOOKMARKED TITLES

Virginia Woolf's *Mrs. Dalloway*
by Robin Black

Middlemarch and the Imperfect Life
by Pamela Erens

James Baldwin's *Another Country*
by Kim McLarin

Truman Capote's *In Cold Blood*
by Justin St. Germain

Vladimir Nabokov's *Speak, Memory*
by Sven Birkerts

William Stoner and the Battle for the Inner Life
by Steve Almond

Stephen King's "The Body"
by Aaron Burch

Raymond Carver's *What We Talk About When We Talk About Love*
by Brian Evenson

(For a complete series list, go to
https://www.igpub.com/category/titles/bookmarked/)